King
The Man Af

by Samuel Ridout

(1855-1930)

For more great Christian classics that have been
out-of-print for far too long, visit us online at:

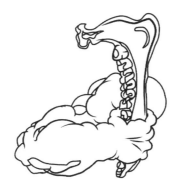

JawboneDigital.com

ISBN: 1546984259
ISBN-13: 978-1546984252

TABLE OF CONTENTS

TABLE OF CONTENTS
(CONTINUED)

PREFACE

The following pages, begun several years ago, and now, in the mercy of God, completed, are an effort to give a brief series of notes upon the first book of Samuel. The title, <u>King Saul: The Man After the Flesh</u>, shows us the central figure of the book, a type too of the fleshly condition of the nation as a whole.

The lessons connected with the rise, reign and end of King Saul are many, and all point to the utter unprofitableness of the flesh in its greatest excellence to be aught that is acceptable to God.

The subject in one sense is a depressing one, and the proper effect should be to turn us from the contemplation of the man after the flesh to the man after God's own heart, David, who comes upon the scene in the latter part of the book and shows the contrast between faith and nature. As a type of Christ, he is the antidote to the baleful example and influence of poor Saul, and thus shows how God would ever lead, even through the knowledge of sin in ourselves and of the evil about us, not to occupation with that, but with Him who is the Deliverer of His people. May the Lord use this effort to trace the workings of the flesh and the triumphs of His grace to the blessing of His people!

A word of explanation may not be out of place as to the character of Jonathan spoken of in the body of the book. The matter is one of great delicacy, and the writer shrinks from taking the edge off any wholesome lessons that have been connected with the character and position of Jonathan, but would only call attention to what is said in the body of the book and leave each reader free to draw his own conclusions.

INTRODUCTORY

In a certain sense, a king is the product of the times in which he lives. He represents the thought and condition of the masses, and while he may be beyond the individuals composing the nation, he will represent the ideal, which they exhibit but partially in their several lives. The king, though above the masses, must be one of themselves, only a greater. Just as the gods of the heathen are but the personification of their own desires and passions enlarged.

In a similar way, every man is a representation of the world at large—a microcosm. He is a sample, as we might say, of the whole, having certain characteristics in greater or less proportion, certain ones obscured by the overshadowing prominence of others; but all features which compose the mass as a whole, present in greater or less degree. It is a solemn thought, and illustrative of our Lord's words to Nicodemus, "That which is born of the flesh is flesh."

We are now looking simply at the natural man and from a natural standpoint. Every observant and thoughtful man will confirm what has been said. Water will not rise higher than its source, and the great leaders of men have been but great men, like the rest of their fellows, only with enlarged capacities and greater force. In fact, the world would boast of the truth of this, and glory in the fact that their great ones are but the exhibition of the qualities that mark all. They make demigods out of their heroes, and then claim kinship with them, thus climbing higher and exalting themselves. It is man's effort to make good the lie of the serpent, "Ye shall be as gods."

It need hardly be said that there is a distinct limit to all this greatness. Between man and God there is still the "great gulf" impossible to pass. Nor is this merely the gulf between creature and Creator, fixed eternally, and which it is the joy of the child of God to recognize—for our happiness is in keeping the creature place of subjection and of infinite inferiority to "God over all blessed forever"—but sin has made the impassable gulf between man and the true knowledge of God. All his development, knowledge, excellence and greatness is on the side away from God, and every fresh instance of human greatness but emphasizes the fact that man is away from God. "Ye must be born again."

Looking, then, at this mass of humanity, "alienated from the life of God"—solemn and awful thought—we see here and there, towering above the rest, some prominent and striking character who naturally attracts our attention. Opportunity, ability, force of character, have separately or unitedly put him in the place of eminence. It will surely give us a clearer idea of humanity to study it in this more excellent form, just as the mineralogist would seek for the richest specimen of ore to determine the quality of the entire deposit. Having found that, he would then remember that this was the best, the rest not yielding so much as his specimen.

So we take up the great men of earth to see what is in man. We take the best specimen, where natural character, opportunity and education have combined to produce the nearest approach to perfection, and having learned thus what he is, we remember that the mass of humanity are but poor specimens of the same class. We will have to confess with the psalmist that "every man at his best state is vanity."

Nor must we leave out the religious element in all this, but rather expect to find it prominent. Man is a religious being, and we will see where his religion leads. This may be a religion based upon God's revelation, and in outward connection with the ordinances of His own establishment. It may make "a fair show" in all this, and under the influence of God-given ministry seem well nigh to have reached the true knowledge of God, and be born anew. We will find food for most solemn thought in all this.

Such a man was king Saul, the ideal of the times in which he lived, and combining in himself traits of character which all admire, and all possess in some degree. Added to this natural excellence, he was the

3

favored son of a favored nation, with abundant opportunities for the knowledge of God, both by revelation and prophecy. He will be found to have possessed in himself those qualities of ability and excellence most admired by man, and added to them the nearest approach, at least, to the true knowledge of God. It will be our duty to decide, so far as man can decide, whether he was in any measure a true subject of grace.

But we have said that every man is but a specimen of the mass—possessing in greater measure what are the common characteristics of all. We can thus get help in determining the character of Saul by seeing the general state of the nation, more particularly at the time just prior to his reign; and our knowledge of Saul will in turn enable us more fully to put a just estimate upon the people.

We must also remember that Israel was representative of the whole human family. A vine was taken out of Egypt and planted in a fruitful hill, surrounded by a hedge and tilled with all the skill of a divine husbandman. He asks, "What could have been done more in My vineyard, than I have done in it?" (Isaiah 5:4.) But it was a natural vine. It was simply the vine of earth given every opportunity to show what fruit it could produce. Saul was a representative Israelite, and Israel was but the best nation of earth. We, therefore, and all humanity, are under review in this examination of king Saul.

So far we have looked merely at the natural man, leaving out of view that gracious work of God which imparts a new life and gives new relationships with Himself. This has doubtless gone on from the time of the fall; God has always had His children—"the sons of God" in the midst of an apostate, godless world. These, His children, have been born of the Spirit, and faith has ever been the characteristic of their life. Whatever the dispensation or the circumstances, faith has been the mark of the people of God, those possessed of life from Him.

We find, therefore, in the history of Israel, no matter how dark the days and how great the apostasy, a remnant of the true people of God who still held fast to Him. It will be for us also to trace the workings of this faith which marks out God's people from the mass of humanity; and here too we will find, no matter how bright the individual instance may be, that this divine life has a character common to all the saints of God. We may see it very clearly in a Hannah, and very dimly in an Eli; but there will be the same life in each. To trace this in contrast to the activities and excellences of the natural man will help us to understand each more clearly.

But here again we will find that our subject is more than a question of persons. We will find that in the same person both these principles may exist, and that this will explain the feebleness of manifestation of the divine life in some, and apparent inconsistencies in all. We will find, and Scripture confirms the truth, that the nature of man remains unchanged—flesh remains that, and spirit also remains spirit; "that which is born of the flesh is flesh; and that which is born of the Spirit is spirit."

May we not, then, expect real profit from this study of Israel's first king? Should it not give us a clearer view of the helpless and hopeless condition of the natural man, of the utter incorrigibility of "the flesh" in the believer, and enable us to discern more accurately than ever between these two natures in the people of God? Thus we would answer more fully to the apostle's description of the true circumcision: "who worship by the Spirit of God, and rejoice in Christ Jesus and have no confidence in the flesh."

Lastly, we will more fully understand the dispensational situation, and see how fully is illustrated the fact that all things wait necessarily for God's true King, for the Man after His own heart, of whom David was the type. King may succeed king, but it will be but the ever varying forms of human excellence as displayed in king Saul. Alas! the true King did come, and the people desired one of the class of Saul—a Barabbas—rather than the True, for their king is but the expression of their own heart and life. Therefore it is only the "righteous nation" who will desire and have that King who shall "reign in righteousness."

PART ONE

CHAPTER 1
THE STATE OF THE PEOPLE

In contrast with the book of Judges, and its supplement Ruth, the books of the Kings deal largely with the national center and the nation as connected with that, and a responsible head. The previous books had given the history of individuals and of separate portions of the nation. While the victories of the judges benefited the people at large, there does not seem to be that cohesion, or that recognition of a divine center, so clearly provided for in the book of Deuteronomy. It is significant that the first allusion to Shiloh, in the book of Judges, is the mention of an idolatrous rival in the tribe of Dan (Judges 18:31).

The book of Samuel begins with Shiloh, and shows us the state of things there, as Judges had shown the general condition of the people. We have in the earlier chapters the state of the priesthood, in Eli and his sons. We might have hoped that, spite of national unfaithfulness, the priests, whose nearness to God was their special privilege, would remain faithful to Him. Alas for man! Be he never so near outwardly, and entrusted with the most priceless privileges, there is nothing in him to bind his heart to God. All must come from God alone; His grace must keep us, or we will not be kept.

There is no such thing as succession in grace. The son of the most faithful father needs to be born again as well as the most degraded of mankind. This is written clearly on many a page of the word of God. "Ye must be born again."

Eli, the high-priest, was personally righteous and loyal in heart to God, but he was weak. This is bad enough in any position, but when one is entrusted with the priesthood of a nation, responsible to maintain them in relationship with God, it is a crime. Eli's sons were godless men without conscience, and yet in the priests' place, and one of them successor to the high-priesthood.

The carelessness of Eli is so dreadful that nothing but the tragic circumstances of his and his sons' death, can fittingly express God's judgment. We will look at that later. We turn now to something brighter.

God has always had a remnant among His people, even in darkest days, and it is most refreshing to see in Hannah a faith and a desire in lovely contrast with Eli's feebleness, and his sons' wickedness. She lays hold of God, and spite of nature's impotence, and the discouragement of a reproof from Eli, she holds fast. What a reproach to Eli! He has no energy to control his wicked house, and therefore has no discernment in administering reproof outside.

Faith may wait and weep, but it has its joys later on, and in Hannah's song of praise we get fresh encouragement to pray and wait. "They that sow in tears shall reap in joy." This remains ever true, for the individual saint and for the Lord's people at any time, and more particularly is it applicable to the remnant in the latter days who will in affliction stay themselves upon the Lord.

This narrative of Hannah gives us a glimpse of what may not have been entirely uncommon among the people, while the mass was in a state of declension. There were always, even in the darkest days, the Lord's "hidden ones," the salt of the earth who preserved the mass from utter corruption for a time at least. It is a comfort to think of this, and to remember that there is at the present time also, a remnant whose heart is turned to the Lord.

But this remnant was not among the official class. The leaders were either too weak or corrupt to help the people. There could be no relief through the ordinary channels, and God must therefore come in by a new way. Samuel, the child of this faith of the remnant, is the first of the prophets.

The prophet was God's special means of communication with the people when the ordinary means had failed. This explains why the message was largely one of sadness. God will intervene; He loves His people too much not to deal with them, but that dealing must be according to His nature and their condition. The presence therefore of the prophet tells the true condition of the people.

Hannah herself is practically a prophetess—all subsequent prophecy is foreshadowed in her song. She exults in the Lord over the conquest of her enemies; she celebrates the holiness of God and His stable purposes of mercy for His people. She rebukes the pride and arrogance of the scoffer, and rejoices in the overthrow of the mighty. The rich have been brought low and the needy lifted up. The barren has become the joyful mother of children. The Lord humbles and exalts—He is sovereign. His adversaries will be overthrown, and His King and His Christ shall be exalted.

Faith looks on ever to the end. If for a time there seem to be partial recovery, still faith does not rest until God can rest. Thus the prophets in a certain sense were not reformers. They accepted and rejoiced in a true turning to God, but they were not deceived by appearances. All reform was but partial and temporary, to be succeeded by still greater darkness. All things wait the coming of the King. He is the desire of all nations, and all who are awakened to see the true condition of the world and of the professed people of God, know there is no hope but in the coming of the Lord.

So too in the history of the individual, whether for salvation or deliverance, there is no expectation from the natural man. The eye of faith is turned from all human excellence to the Christ of God. What peace of soul, what Hannah-like exultation of spirit there is, when He is the object! Christ alone the Savior; Christ alone the One in whom is deliverance from the power of sin.

But this complete setting aside of the flesh in all its forms by Hannah, shows at once her own deliverance and the bondage of the mass of the nation by whom she was surrounded. The people's condition was the very opposite of hers, and their confidence and expectation was in man. In this negative way, then, we may learn the true state of the people,—a state of ease and self-sufficiency on the part of many, of more or less open enmity to God, and a weak, helpless sense of need on the part of those partially aroused to the true condition of things.

The state was similar, under altered circumstances, in the days just preceding our Lord's advent. Then too there was a feeble remnant which stayed itself upon God, and a self-satisfied, hypocritical class of rulers, who led the people as they wished. Then, too, faith waited for divine consolation, and was rewarded with a sight of the wondrous Babe of whose coming Hannah's song spoke. She could well have mingled her praises with those of Mary. But how few felt the need which had been satisfied in those few who had turned entirely from themselves to God and His remedy.

Returning for a little, we must look at the state of the people as exemplified in that of the priests, for as the Scripture shows, the one corresponds to the other. "The prophets prophesy falsely, and the priests bear rule by their means; and My people love to have it so" (Jeremiah 5:31). Here we see the false prophets, claiming to reveal God's mind, and the priests bearing rule by this. But such a state would be impossible were the people not willing. The people, if only outwardly connected with God, are glad to have a carnal priesthood. So in the history of the professing church, with the awful iniquity of the priests, we must remember that it was but the reflection of the state of a carnal people; in name only the people of God. No doubt a godly priest would do much to check the abounding evil of the people, and a godless one would accelerate their decline. Hence, the solemn responsibility of those in such a place. But the point of importance to remember is that a people away from God make possible a wicked priesthood, as the latter intensifies the alienation of the people.

But what a picture of reckless blasphemy and grossest wickedness have we in these priests. One bears the honored name of a faithful predecessor and relative Phinehas, "the mouth of brass." The name is suggestive of what he was, an unyielding witness for God in a day of apostasy and corruption, who by his faithfulness wrought righteousness, stayed the plague and obtained "an everlasting priesthood," as type of the Priest who one day will put down all evil and maintain abiding relationship between God and His people (Numbers 25:7-13). With this one, however, nothing remains but the name. Is it not suggestive also that Eli was not a descendent of Phinehas, but of Ithamar, the other son of Aaron? So that at this time, for some reason, the proper line of descent had not been observed, which in itself may indicate the disordered condition of everything. For Phinehas had been promised an abiding priesthood, "A mouth of brass" indeed had this younger Phinehas, but not on God's behalf, as a faithful witness for Him. Rather, he hardened himself against God, and would be one of those who would say, "Our lips are our own; who is lord over us?"

Hophni, too, while there is no historical connection with his name, seems to answer to it only in an evil way. "My hands," seems to be the meaning, which some have thought to suggest "fighter." But the root with which it is connected is used for describing the hands as capable of holding, rather than of striking. Very noticeably it is applied to the priest entering the holiest on the day of atonement, "with his hands full of sweet incense" (Leviticus 16:12). It would thus be a good priestly name, and fitting companion for Phinehas. "Hands full" of incense and an unyielding testimony. Alas, the hands of Hophni were full, but not of the materials of praise. They were filled with ill-gotten gain and the fat of the Lord's offerings appropriated to his own use. The sin of these men was twofold, the one resulting from the other. In the judgment of the world they would not have seemed equally heinous. They were guilty of sacrilege and of gross immorality, the latter a fitting consequence of the former.

And is not this always the case? Where God is displaced, His service despised, is not the relation between man and man also corrupted? The unspeakable corruption described in the early part of Romans is the direct result of man's turning from God. So here. The priests will have their own part out of the sacrifice—not that in mercy provided for them in the law of God, but of the best, and of that which belonged to Him alone. When the worshipers, with some remains of a tender conscience, would plead that God have His part first, the rough answer and threatened violence was all the satisfaction they could get. Thus the Lord's offering was despised, and the sin of the priests was "very great before the Lord."

If there is one form of sin more abhorrent than another, and which will bring more fearful punishment, it is that which disports itself in the presence of holy things. This is why religious corruption is the worst. The conscience is seared, and God's holy name is dragged into the most unholy associations. Will He allow it? Ah, He will no more allow it in a formal, Christ-less church than He would in a formal Israel. Men despised holy things, because of their abuse by the priests. And is it not true, not only in Rome past and present, but in the professing church today, that the world despises divine things because those who should be "holy priests," do not give God the chief place in their professed service of Him? When people cease to fear before God, when they see in His ministers mere selfish disregard of God's will, we have apostasy. It is not extravagant to say that such is largely the condition in Christendom today. The Lord's offering is despised.

Eli hears of all his sons' wickedness and calls them to account. His words are strong and good. But of what avail are good and strong words when the strong arm of judgment should fall? The law provided the penalty for such sacrilege as this, in death. Why did not Eli show himself to be truly zealous for the Lord's honor? Ah, words, mere words no matter how strong are worse than guilty complicity. Worse, for the man who utters them knows the evil and goes on with it.

There is solemn instruction in this. It is not enough to see the wrong of a thing, or even to bear witness against it. Action is necessary. This is why so many—Lot like—fret and talk against evil and find no relief or help. Action must be taken, either by inflicting true discipline upon the evil-doer, or, if this be impossible, by separation from a state of things which makes it impossible. Otherwise men will be engulfed in the judgment of the very thing against which they so loudly declaim.

This may seem harsh, but it is in accord with the witness of the man of God who is sent to Eli. He associates Eli with his sons: "wherefore kick ye at My sacrifice and at My offering…and honorest thy sons above Me, to make yourselves fat with the chiefest of all the offerings of Israel My people!" Not one word of commendation for his own faithfulness, or personal piety. "Them that honor Me, I will honor." And so Eli and his house go down in a common dishonor, branded with the common shame of having despised the Lord. Would that the lesson of this could be fully learned. "Let every one that nameth the name of Christ depart from iniquity."

It is refreshing and yet most sad to think of the child Samuel growing up in an atmosphere like this. Refreshing, for the Lord kept him inviolate amidst "the obscene tumult which raged all around;" but sad that one so tender should not only witness, but be obliged to witness against this awful state of things. "But Samuel ministered before the Lord, being a child, girded with a linen ephod." "And the child Samuel grew on, and was in favor both with the Lord, and also with men." "And the child Samuel ministered unto the Lord before Eli" (1 Samuel 2:18, 26; 3:1). The mention of the ephod, the priestly garment, would suggest that on a little child had fallen the only spotless robe in the priesthood. He represents, as we might say, for the time being, the house of Aaron, fallen into ruins in the hands of Eli and his sons. The child grew on and ministered to the Lord before Eli.

Be he but a child, no one who is truly before God will be long without a message from God. So Samuel gets his first revelation from the One till then but dimly known by him. Poor Eli! Eyesight has well nigh gone, as well as faithfulness, and lying down to slumber he fittingly suggests the spiritual state he was in. How hopeless, to human appearances, was the state. How unlikely that God would intervene. And yet it is just then that He does speak, and to a little child. Thrice He must call before it dawns upon Eli that the Lord is speaking to the child. He had told him to "go and lie down again," even as many careless ones would seek to quiet those to whom God is speaking. But at last it dawns upon the old man that it is God who is there, and he dare not—weak as he may be with his sons—he would not silence that Voice, slow as he had been to obey it.

How touching and interesting is the scene which follows, familiar to every Christian child. What a moment in this child's life—God, the living God, deigns to call and to speak with him. What an honor; how lovely and yet how solemn. Well may the child say "Speak Lord for Thy servant heareth."

But what a message for a child's ears. Why should this awful story of sin and its judgment be the first words which the Lord should speak to the little one? Does it not emphasize for us the fact that the judgment of sin is as necessary for the young as the old? And that God's messenger in a world like this must hear all His word? How many plead that they are not suited for such testimony. They love to hear the sweet and precious things of the gospel, but when it comes to the solemn declarations as to the state of the Church and the path for faith, how many plead that they are not ready for such things. A child can hear and declare the message of God.

We can think of that little lad, lying open-eyed till the morning, with the great awe of God's nearness upon him; and naturally shrinking from the responsibility of declaring this message to Eli. He quietly opens the doors of the Lord's house—significant act—fearing to speak of what he had heard. But Eli calls him, and, faithful to himself, if not to his sons, hears and bows to the awful sentence of God pronounced by the lips of a child.

When once God lays hold of an instrument, working upon the heart as well as the mind, He will doubtless continue to make use of it. So Samuel not only received the first message of judgment upon Eli's house, but was made the channel of God's resumed relationship with the people. "The Lord appeared again in Shiloh: for the Lord revealed Himself to Samuel in Shiloh, by the word of the Lord."

What an honor—to be used of God, after ruin had come into the very household of the priest. And is it not true that at this day, God passes by all pretentious officialism which has departed from Him, to reveal to babes the things hidden from the wise and prudent? The childlike, obedient spirit, which can say, "Speak Lord, for Thy servant heareth," will have a message.

Nor will the humble instrument fail of recognition, though the careless and thoughtless may mock. The Lord let none of his words fall to the ground; what he said came to pass, and his message commanded a respect which could not be withheld. The words spoken to Jeremiah are also appropriate to him: "Say not, I am a child: for thou shalt go to all that I send thee, and whatsoever I command thee thou shalt speak. Be not afraid of their faces; for I am with thee to deliver thee, saith the Lord. Behold I have put My words in thy mouth" (Jeremiah 1:7-9). No need to fear the face of man when one has seen the face of God. The weakest is as the mighty when he has the words of God on his lips. Let us remember this in these days, and faint not because of our feebleness. The Lord will let none of His words fall to the ground, though spoken by faltering lips.

We have seen now the state of the people. The mass, weak, prone to wander, and, without the strong hand of restraint, lapsing into carelessness and idolatry; the priestly family degenerated into senile feebleness and youthful profligacy; but, in the midst of all this, a feeble, prayerful remnant who still count upon God, and obtain His recognition. This remnant finds expression, in God's mercy, through the gift of prophecy, raised up by Him as a witness against the abounding apostasy, and the channel of His dealings with the people. Sad and dark days they were, but just the time for faith to shine out brightly and to do valiantly for the Lord.

CHAPTER 2
THE CAPTIVITY IN THE PHILISTINES' LAND

1 Samuel 4

As has been frequently noticed, the enemy who could successfully attack the people of God, represent in a spiritual way their state, or the natural consequence of their state. Throughout Judges we find various enemies, assailing different parts of the nation and at different times. At one time it is the Moabites on the east; at another, Jabin king of Hazor on the north. The first suggests carnal profession, and the second rationalism. The last enemy spoken of in Judges was the Philistines. Samson, last, strongest and feeblest of the judges, fought against them during his life—when he was not having associations with them. He did much, in an indefinite way, to keep them from completely bringing the people into bondage, but never wrought a thorough deliverance. He died in captivity, and though he slew at his death more than he had in his life, he left them still practically unconquered.

These are the enemies that confront Israel during the priesthood of Hophni and Phinehas, and all through the reign of Saul. So we must see afresh what they represent in a spiritual way. Living in the territory which rightly belonged to Israel—their own land—they stand for that which is closest to the people of God without being really such. They drifted into the land—exemplifying their name, "wanderers,"—along the shore of the Mediterranean sea, the short way from Egypt. For them there was need neither of the sheltering passover, the opened Red Sea or Jordan's flow arrested. They stand thus for the natural man intruding into the things of God.

That this has been done in its full measure by Rome, none can question. She has taken possession of the heritage of God's people, and settled there as though it belonged by right to her, giving her name to the entire Church, or claiming to be "the Church," just as Palestine, the whole land, got its name from these Philistines. Rome with its profession, its ritualism remains the great enemy which menaces the inheritance of the saints. It is to be feared that Protestantism, like Samson, has but feebly dealt with this adversary, and too often adopted its principles to be a true and victorious deliverer from it. They still remain in probably greater vigor than ever, ready to make fresh inroads and to lay waste more of the land of God's people.

But Rome as a system appeals to man's carnal nature. It may be said that all mere carnal, formal religion is Rome in principle. At any rate, doubtless, the Philistines stand for all that is of nature in the things of God. Any carnal trafficking in unfelt, unrealized truth is but the intrusion of the flesh—mere Philistinism. This explains the constant tendency toward ritualism, and so toward Rome. Nor will this cease till the "mother of harlots" gathers back her children, representing apostate Christendom, after the removal of the Church to heaven. Rome will again be supreme.

A state of the people like that which we have been tracing, with its carnal and corrupt priesthood and no power to act for God, would be just suited for the degradation now imminent. Indeed in Hophni and Phinehas we see but Philistines under another name. God will show His people outwardly where they are inwardly. How often in the individual soul, and in the Church at large, are the outward sins but the expression of a state of heart which has long existed.

We are not told the occasion of the conflict here, whether there was some fresh inroad of the enemy, some additional imposition of tyranny, or whether in fancied strength the people arrayed themselves against them. This last would almost seem likeliest from the language, "Israel went out against the Philistines to battle." "Pride goeth before destruction," and self-sufficiency is ever the sign of an absence of self-judgment. Many times do God's people go out to do battle against a spiritual foe in a state of soul which would make victory impossible, which it would really compromise God's honor were He to give it. This is why it is absolutely imperative that there should be the judgment of self, before there can be a true warfare against outward foes.

But one defeat is not enough to teach the people their need, and the folly of their course. Four thousand fall before the enemy, and surely this should have brought them on their faces in confession and prayer to know the reason of this defeat. Had they waited upon God, they would soon have learned the reason, and doubtless have been spared the further loss of the next battle. But evidently they think nothing of their own condition, and the only remedy they can think of is truly a Philistine one. They will have something outward and visible brought along which will quicken the failing courage of the people, and strike terror into the hearts of their enemy. It does both, for when the ark is brought into the camp, a great shout is raised by Israel, and the Philistines are smitten with fear.

The ark had led them to victory before. It had gone before them in the wilderness, "to search out a resting-place"; it had stopped Jordan for them to pass over, and had led them about Jericho till its walls fell. Naturally they think of it as the very throne of God, and substitute it, in their minds, for God Himself.

But God is holy, and can never be made to link His name with unholiness. The ark was His resting-place in Israel, but He cannot be forced to countenance sin. So His ark can no more overthrow the enemy than Israel could previously. The hosts of Israel are overthrown, Hophni and Phinehas are slain, the ark is taken captive, and carried in triumph and placed in the house of Dagon, thus giving the glory of the victory to the idol.

What food for solemn thought is here. No outward privilege, no past experiences of God's presence, no correctness of position or doctrine can take the place of reality of soul before God. None can ever say they have a claim upon God because of any thing except Christ Himself laid hold of, and presented in true self-distrust and brokenness, with real, true judgment of all in the life that would dishonor the Lord.

This is the meaning of "Ichabod," the glory has departed. It refers to the ark, the glory of God's manifest presence; but this can only abide among a broken, self-judged people. In a real sense, we have the Spirit of God always abiding with us, but if that is allowed in the heart or life which grieves Him, all outward and manifest approval of God ceases. He will permit the badge of His presence to be removed. Persons will lose the joy of the Lord individually, and the candlestick of collective testimony be removed, if God's warnings fail to bring His people into their true place. Let us ponder this lesson, remembering that none have a claim for permanent recognition, but only as God's holy presence is not dishonored.

Poor Eli! He had died long before, so far as service for God was concerned. His lesson is written large and clear. May we have grace to learn it. The way to "Ichabod" is careless weakness when God's honor is involved. He bears patiently, but there is a limit to His forbearance, and when there is "no remedy," He must allow the due results of His people's weakness, folly and unfaithfulness.

So far as the people were concerned, they had lost the very badge of their relationship with God. "The Ark of the Covenant" had passed from their unfaithful hands—the very throne of God was no longer in Israel. "He forsook the tabernacle of Shiloh, the tent which He placed among men; and delivered His strength into captivity, and His glory into the enemy's hand" (Psalm 78:60-61).

What an abiding witness that God will never act contrary to His nature, even though the stability of His earthly throne seem for a time to be threatened.

How it shows that all divine power is holy, and that there is no authority save that which is consistent with God's holiness. God does not need to preserve the outward continuity of His government, as is the common thought of men. What a mass of ecclesiastical rubbish is swept aside when this is seen. No need to delve into the annals of the past—doctrinal errors of the early "Fathers," grossest abuses of Rome, with her rival popes and councils, all tainted with that unholiness which forever disqualifies them from a claim to God's recognition. No need to search here for a succession from the apostles. Ichabod is upon it all. God forsook all that, as He did Shiloh of old.

But what a relief is this to see that God can never be held responsible for the errors of His professed people. Were this seen, how quickly would earnest souls turn from Rome or any other establishment which bases its claims of authority upon an unholy past. God can never act contrary to His character, and when that character has been distinctly and persistently ignored, we have a Shiloh—no matter what precious associations may be linked with it —bereft of its glory. Faith can follow God. Even as at an earlier day, when the golden calf usurped God's place in Israel, Moses pitched the tent of meeting outside the camp, and thither resorted all who desired to meet Jehovah, rather than the place where once He manifested Himself.

Thus faith ever reasons: "Let us go forth unto Him without the camp." Has He been compelled to withdraw? We can no longer recognize that which He has left. Shiloh with the ark away is like a body when the spirit has departed. It can only be buried out of our sight.

We have here a principle of wide-reaching application. Not only is a simple path for faith laid down, where there is no need to attempt to justify what is not of God but there is a basis here for recovery to Him, and thus for true unity amongst His people. Who would not desire that? But it can only be in this way.

The great mistake with nearly all efforts after outward unity among God's people, is in having the eye upon them rather than upon Him. The question, the only question to be asked is: Where is God with reference to the matters upon which His people are divided? Has He been compelled to withdraw His approval? Does His word condemn that which characterizes His people? To uphold their position does that need to be maintained which violates, in a radical way, His character? Then surely all effort at uniting His people, and at the same time ignoring that which has dishonored God, will never meet with His approval, not even if it outwardly brought together all those now separated. God, His will, His character, ignored—all else is absolutely worthless.

But have not all here a most simple basis of true unity? We side with God—we take up, patiently and prayerfully, if painfully, that which has occasioned the breach. Is it a matter about which God's word expresses His mind? Then the only thing to be done is to own that mind—to bow to Him. On the other hand, is it a matter practically immaterial, where patience and forbearance would accomplish what suspicion and force could not do? Then the path is equally clear. May there ever be grace among His own to seek to be with God according to His word, and they will ever be with one another also. Mere ebullition of love to saints, no matter how real, can never take the place of a clear, thorough examination of the difficulties in the light of God's word. To ignore difficult questions, is but to invite fresh and more hopeless complications. But we must return to our narrative.

CHAPTER 3
GOD'S CARE FOR HIS OWN HONOR

1 Samuel 5–6

Having thus vindicated the holiness of His character by permitting the ark to be removed from Shiloh, and taken captive by the Philistines, God will now show to its very captors that His power and majesty is unchanged. We need never be afraid that God will fail to vindicate either His holiness or His power. Our only fear should be lest we be not in that state in which we can be vessels of testimony for Him.

Notice how all interest is transferred from Israel to the Philistines' land. Wherever God's presence is must be the true center of interest. Nor does this mean that God has permanently forsaken Israel or ceased to love them. Nay, all that is now transpiring in the distant land is but the twofold preparation for the maintenance of His holiness and His grace toward a repentant people.

The Philistines have looked upon this capture of the ark not only as their victory over Israel, but over God as well. They ascribe both to their own god, Dagon, and in acknowledgement of his triumph over Israel's God, they put the ark in Dagon's temple.

It is now no longer a question between God and Israel, or even between God and the Philistines, but between the true God and man's false one—part fish, part man, as the perverted and corrupt ingenuity of fallen man delights to depict the god of his own fashioning. This false god is at once immeasurably inferior to man, like to the fish in the main, with head and hands of human intelligence and power, and yet the object of his dread and worship. Such is the idol ever, in all its forms, really beneath those who form it.

At first, doubtless to impress more fully the lesson, God simply casts the image prostrate before Him. Poor hardened man sets it up again. But the second time, the blindness of the people failing to understand, Dagon falls and is broken. He loses all that had given him a semblance of intelligence or power, and the headless trunk witnesses of the vanity of idols, and of the majesty and power of that God whom they in their madness had despised.

Had there been the least desire after truth, what an effectual witness would this have been to the Philistines of the vanity of Dagon and the reality of the living God! Alas, their hardened hearts see but little in it, and give added honor to Dagon by not treading upon the threshold, where his head and hands had lain. Doubtless the priests put head and hands back again, and most was soon forgotten. How utterly hopeless is all witness to those who do not desire to know the truth. But God is vindicated, and His desire as well to deliver men from their errors.

In how many ways does Rome answer to all this persistent and shameless idolatry. Dagon, the fish-god, suggests that worship of increase, for which the fish is remarkable, and which forms one of Rome's claims to "Catholic." Does she not number her adherents by millions?

Nor can we fail to recognize in all our hearts that Philistine tendency to worship numbers. Is it not the test of a work? How many simply follow a multitude, and measure all spiritual results by the number of those who are identified with a movement. Again and again does God break to pieces this false god, permitting the loss of hands and feet—both intelligence and power to that which a carnal religion would still deify. We need to have this thing hunted out of our souls. Mere numbers are no token of God's presence or approval, whether it be in evangelistic work or any testimony for God. His truth must ever be the test—His word, as applied by His Spirit. Without that it is but Dagon.

God's judgment is not confined to the overthrow of Dagon; He will touch not merely the idolatry of the people, but their prosperity and lives as well. As He had previously in Egypt not only-poured out His plagues upon the people, but upon their sources of livelihood, so He does here. His hand was laid heavily upon them and He smote them with emerods, a plague similar, probably, to the boils of Egypt and to what is now known as the Bubonic plague, repulsive and deadly in its effects. He had said: "Against all the gods of Egypt I will execute judgment" (Exodus 12:12), making the infliction so sweeping that neither people nor gods could ever again be pointed to as having been immune. So He would do in the land of the Philistines, no less effectually, if on a smaller scale, stopping every possible opportunity for unbelief to lift its head again.

And do we not see mercy in all this? Had Dagon merely been overthrown, the unbelief of the people and their half pity for their god would have found some ready excuse which would have enabled them to patch up their pride and their wounded god at the same time and go on with the old idolatry but if the judgment affects their property as well, and if the little mice, so contemptibly insignificant, can yet ravage their fields so as to rob them of the staff of life, they are forced to acknowledge here a hand whose weight they begin to feel and from under whose chastening they cannot escape. And when the blow comes still nearer and the stroke of God is felt upon their own bodies, with the dead all about them, surely they must be compelled to bow and own the rod.

So God's judgments are designed, if there be the least vestige of submission to Him, the least desire to turn from wickedness to Himself, to break down the pride and unbelief of the heart. This is the effect of all chastening upon those who are properly exercised thereby: "What son is he whom the father chasteneth not?" God's people from the beginning have been acquainted with the rod, and how many have had occasion to bless Him infinitely for the overthrow of idols which they had set up, the loss of property, of health, yea even of this life itself! May we not all say: "I know, Lord, that in faithfulness Thou hast afflicted," and add: "It is good for me that I have been afflicted. Before I was afflicted, I went astray, but now have I kept Thy word"?

So God was not merely vindicating His own honor, but had they only known it, was speaking in no uncertain way, in mercy, to the godless nation among whom He had permitted His glory to be brought. What an opportunity indeed for repentance we might almost say what a necessity for it. And yet, alas, it was unavailed of showing how hopelessly and permanently alienated from any desire toward Himself were the Philistines, who, like the other nations cast out by Joshua, had filled up the measure of that iniquity which, in the days of Abraham, God in His patience had declared not yet full, and whom indeed it would be a mercy to sweep from the land.

And as we look at the world about us, under both the goodness and the severity of God, receiving His blessings, and experiencing the weight of His hand in providential dealings, do we not see how all this is calculated both to lead man to think of God and to repentance? Will it not be a weighty item in that awful account which the world must one day face? Particularly is this true in Christendom, where the light of revelation and the gospel of God's grace alike serve to illumine all that is darkest in His providence. Men will be without excuse. The very plea that they sometimes make, that for one who has had so much suffering in this life there must surely be a relief in the life to come, will but give added solemnity to the awful doom. If they had suffering in this life—trial, privation, bereavement, sickness, what effect did it have upon them? Did it bring them to see the vanity of earthly things, the uncertainty of life, the power of God, and above all their own sin before Him? Did it drive them to Christ, if they would not be wooed and drawn by the love of God? Oh, what an awful reckoning for the world! Woe to those indeed upon whom neither the love and mercy of God, nor the smiting of His hand have any effect!

At least, however, His own honor and His own goodness are vindicated. Men will not be able to say that God did not make His presence manifested. They will not be able to say that the sun of prosperity shone so uninterruptedly that they were never forced to think of eternal things. God's cup indeed is "full of mixture," and the mercy and the judgment alike vindicate His ways and show that deep desire of His heart, "Who will have all men to be saved and to come to the knowledge of the truth." Such lessons, surely, we are warranted in gathering from this judgment upon the Philistines, though undoubtedly the main lesson was for His redeemed people. To bring upon them a deeper sense of their own unfaithfulness, and to show the power and holiness of God unchanged, were the primary objects.

What Israelite, as he looked back at the defeat at Ebenezer (1 Samuel 4:1), with the ark carried off in triumph by the Philistines, and then at prostrate Dagon and the plagues upon the Philistines, could fail to learn the lesson so plainly taught? Must he not say, "Our God is holy"—He will not leave His honor to the unclean hands of wicked priests or an ungodly nation. But that which we could not care for, He still maintains.

But how touching it is to think of the desires of our blessed God as manifested in all this judgment on the Philistines! He dwells amid the praises of His people. He cannot dwell in a strange land. His heart is toward them, though in faithfulness He may have had to turn from them and all that went on in Philistia but showed that divine restlessness of love which could not be at peace until it reposed again in the bosom of His redeemed ones. What love we see here! Veiled it may be, but surely not to faith. He will go back to the land from whence He has been driven by the faithlessness of His people, and not by the power of their enemies. He will bestir Himself to return to them if indeed there is a heart to receive Him, but in that divine equipoise of all His attributes His love must not outrun His holiness. Hence the object lesson before the eyes of all.

The nature of these plagues, no doubt, is typical here, as in the similar circumstances in Egypt. The emerods or tumors suggest the outward manifestation of a corruption which had long existed within, and which needed but the opportunity to display itself in all its hideous vileness. How solemnly true it is that to "receive the things done in the body" will be in a very real sense the essence of retribution! "Let him alone" is the most awful sentence that can be pronounced against any, and to allow the hell that is shut up in the heart of every unsaved man to express itself is an awful foretaste of that eternal doom where the knowledge of one's self means the knowledge of sin. True indeed it is that there will be the infliction of wrath also, but will not this be felt in the reaping of what has been sown? "He that is filthy, let him be filthy still." Permanence of character—solemn and awful thought for those who are away from God! The world little realizes, or makes itself easily forget, that beneath the fair exterior of a life no worse than that of most, there is hidden the possibility for every form of sin. It is out of the heart that "proceed evil thoughts, murders, blasphemies," and all the rest. So God was merely letting the wickedness of the wicked be manifest.

So, too, with the mice, as we said, small and contemptible in themselves; who would have thought that those fields of golden grain, with their abundant store, could be devoured by these trifles? So, today, in the world, men despise the trifles as they call them, which one day will eat out all the gladness and peace of life. Socialism, anarchy, various forms of infidelity, disobedience to parents, restiveness under restraint, pride, self-sufficiency—these things are either looked at with toleration, or, if characterized aright, as being so exceptional that there is no danger from them. And yet the book of Revelation traces all these things to the heading up of iniquity. The lawless one is but the embodiment of that lawlessness which even now is working in the children of unbelief. The fearful plagues recorded in that last book of prophecy are but the full development of the little mice, as we might call them, which are even now gnawing out the vitals of society and present order. Once let the powers of evil be turned loose, let the restraining hand of Him who "letteth" be lifted, and He (the Spirit in the Church) be taken away—as will soon come to pass at the coming of the Lord—and the ravages of evil fittingly described as famine and pestilence will show what the world may expect when left to itself. Would to God it had a voice for it now in this the day of His patience!

These inflictions appall the men of Ashdod where the ark had first been brought, and like men in similar case, they try to get rid of the cause, not by repentance, but by putting, as it were, God far off from them. If the load grows too heavy for one shoulder, it will be transferred to the other and then to the arms. It does not become so intolerable that they are prostrated before the God of Israel as yet still less does it have the effect of bringing them to a sense of their true condition. They will get rid of the trouble by getting rid of the ark, and so it is sent on to Gath and from Gath to Ekron, and thus through all the cities of the Philistines.

The same story is repeated everywhere. Men cannot so easily get rid of their chastening, and to shift the burden of an uneasy conscience will not remove the certainty of judgment. This passage of the ark from one city to the other of the Philistines is again a witness of the mercy and of the holiness of God. He will, as it were, knock at the door of each place, even as He did in Sodom, ere judgment fell finally, to see if there would be any that feared Him. And as He passes from one place to the other, we may well believe that there was no response save that of terror, no turning to Himself.

But what a triumphant procession for this ark it was! Even as when Paul passed from one heathen city to another, where Jewish hatred and Gentile scorn vied with each other in heaping reproaches upon him, he could say: "Thanks be to God who always leadeth us in triumph" (as the original has it) "in Christ." Whether it were the stones at Lystra, or the prison at Philippi, or the mockery at Corinth and Athens, faith could see the triumphant witness of the glory of God brought face to face with those people. Even as our Lord, when He sent His disciples through the various cities of Israel, foreseeing their rejection in many places and telling them that they were to shake off the very dust of their feet from those cities where they were not received, added: "Notwithstanding, be ye sure of this, that the Kingdom of God is come nigh unto you." So here, the ark of God makes its majestic progress from city to city, and prostrate forms of men, and devastated garners bear witness to its progress. "The Lord is known by the judgment which He executeth."

At last, desperation drives the lords of the Philistines to a conference in which they decide that what they thought was a victory over Jehovah was but a defeat for themselves; a victory too dearly bought to be longer endured, and they take the world's way (alas, the only way the world will take) of finding relief. They will get rid of God, even as the men of Decapolis besought our Lord to depart out of their coasts, though before their very eyes was the witness of His love and power in setting free the poor demoniac. Yes, the world will try to get rid of God. It may apparently succeed for a season, until the final day.

They decide to return the ark to the land of Israel: "Send away the ark of the God of Israel and let it go again to his own place, that it slay us not and our people; for there was a deadly destruction throughout all the city; the hand of God was very heavy there."

"And the ark of the Lord was in the country of the Philistines seven months"—a complete cycle of time, witnessing perfectly to God's abhorrence of His people's course on the one hand; and, on the other, to the utter helplessness of idolatry to resist Him, or of the unsanctified to endure His presence.

Seven is too familiar a number to need much explanation. Its recurrence, however, in connection with the periods of God's separation from His people and of the infliction of judgments is significant and needs but to be mentioned. A glance at the pages of Daniel and the book of Revelation will make this plain. Is it not significant, too, that the day of atonement came in the seventh month, the time of national humiliation and turning to God marking the beginning of blessing,—a date, in fact, taken as the beginning of the year rather than redemption in the passover of the first month. Redemption is to be entered into, and the humbling truths of sin and helplessness and departure from God on the part of His own to be learned, before there can be the true beginning of that great year which we call the millennium.

Determined now, if possible, to get rid of their plagues and of Him who had inflicted them at the same time, the Philistines cast about for the best way to return the ark to its place without further offending such a God as this. It is significantly characteristic of their utterly unrepentant. condition, that they turned not to Him who had afflicted them for instruction, but to their own priests, those who ministered before Dagon, and to the diviners, corresponding to the magicians of Egypt, who bewitched them and led them astray. How true it is that the natural man never, under any circumstances, will of his own accord turn to the only source of light there is. It is only the child of God, the one divinely and savingly wrought upon by the Spirit of God, who can enter into the word, "Hear ye the rod and Him who hath appointed it." It is to His own people that God says: "If thou wilt return, return unto Me." What can priests or diviners know of the true way in which to deal with God, or to return to Him that which had been taken from Him, His own glory and His throne? Still the divine purpose has been effected and the time for the return of the ark has come. Therefore no fresh judgment marks this further insult, and they are allowed to take the way suggested by the priests, out of which indeed God gets fresh glory to Himself and gives an additional testimony to the fact that He is indeed the only true God.

There is some feeble groping toward divine truth suggested in the advice of the priests and diviners: "If ye send away the ark of the God of Israel, send it not away empty, but anywise return Him a trespass-offering. Then shall ye be healed, and it shall be known to you why His hand is not removed from you" (1 Samuel 6:3). In the darkest mind of the heathen there is a vague, indefinite sense of sin against God. It is, we may well believe, that witness which God leaves in the heart of every man, the most benighted, as well as the most highly cultured, that he has trespassed against his Creator and his Ruler. It is too universal to be ignored. The sense of sin is as wide as the human race, and the sense, too, of the need in some form or other, of a propitiatory offering to God. It takes various forms, the most uncouth and repulsive of the savage, and, no less insulting to

God, the self-satisfied presentation of gifts of good works or reformation on the part of the Christ-less professor.

This trespass-offering, then, which is to be returned with the ark must be at once a memorial of the judgment, and of a value which suggests the reverence due for the One against whom they had trespassed. We notice, however, that the offerings go no further than the memorial of their affliction. Images are made of the emerods and of the mice, but what about that sin which brought this judgment upon them? Is there any confession of that, is there any memorial of that? Ah, no. The natural man sees the affliction and so magnifies that as to forget or ignore the cause for which the affliction came. How different this from the true trespass-offering which alone can avail before a holy God! That which is not so much a memorial of the affliction or judgment deserved as an acknowledgment of the sin which made it necessary; and above all, a confession that the only propitiatory which can be acceptable to God is that unblemished sacrifice of a guiltless substitute, a constantly recurring witness throughout Israel's history and ritual, of Christ, who alone is the trespass-offering, the One who "bare our sins in His own body on the tree."

He has not merely satisfied every demand of God's justice, but in the beautiful teaching of the type, has restored to Him more than was taken away; for the fifth part had to be added to whatever had been stolen. What a joy it is to contemplate this trespass-offering and to know that our acceptance before God is not measured, as we might say, by mere even-handed justice, though divine, but that we are far more the objects of His delight and complacency than we could possibly have been had we never sinned. We are "accepted in the Beloved," thank God. No image, even though it were golden, of our plagues and the sins which made them necessary, but the Image of God Himself, the One in whom shines "all the fulness of the Godhead bodily," and we "complete in Him." How worthless, and in one sense insulting to divine honor, seems this presentation of the golden mice! It was all that poor heathenism could give, all that it could rise to in its conception of what God demanded; nor can this be in the least an excuse for their ignorance, as it was a witness of most absolute and hopeless estrangement from Himself.

And yet we need not travel very far in Christendom to find very much the same spirit at least, amongst those about whose feet shines the light of gospel truth. In the churches of Rome can be seen hundreds of little votive offerings hung upon the walls; crutches, and other evidences of affliction which have been offered to God by those in distress. Nor is it confined to such tawdry trifles as these. In the spiritual realm how much is brought to God of this character! It comes far short, indeed, of His thought, because it comes so far short of Christ Himself.

The priests also appeal to the Philistines to take warning from the similar judgments which had been inflicted upon Pharaoh and the Egyptians. In his blind hatred, Pharaoh knew not what his servants recognized, that the land of Egypt was destroyed, his heart being hardened to his own destruction. The Philistines are warned lest they harden their hearts in the same way. So it is, nature can take warnings and guard its course so as to escape the extreme of judgment, without in the least being softened into true penitence. It is but another form of selfishness that will save itself and take sufficient interest in God's past ways to learn how it can with least danger to itself go on still ignoring and despising Him. An Ahab might walk softly for many years and put off the evil day of reckoning about his murder of Naboth. But Ahab with all his soft walking was Ahab still, unrepentant and hardened, the very goodness of God in sparing him not melting him to repentance, but encouraging him to go on in his course of apostasy. All this is the opposite of that godly sorrow which worketh repentance that needeth not to be repented of.

The lords of the Philistines are willing enough to listen to all this advice, and further, in obedience to their instructions, they prepare the trespass-offering, putting it in a coffer alongside the ark and laying both upon a new cart. Fitting indeed that it should be new, one that had never been used in Philistine service. Instinct often guides those who are most ignorant.

The latent unbelief in the heart of the Philistines is seen in the way they took to restore the ark to the land of Israel. Who would have thought of taking two heifers who had never known the yoke, and harnessing them to a cart without drivers? Would not this insure the destruction of the ark? And to accentuate the difficulty, the calves of these cattle were left behind, so that all nature was against the ark ever reaching the land of Israel. May we not well believe there was a latent hope in the hearts of the people that it would turn out differently from what they were constrained to believe? "If it goeth up by the way of its own coast to Beth-shemesh, then He hath done us this great evil; but if not, then we shall know it was not His hand that smote us; it was a chance that happened to us." Truly, if the living God Himself were not directly concerned in it all, if it were not absolutely His hand that had inflicted the blow on account of the presence of His ark, if it were not His will to restore His throne again to His people, no better means could have been taken to manifest the fact.

But God delights in such opportunities to manifest Himself and to make bare His arm, surely we may well believe a closing witness to the hardened hearts of these people that He was indeed God, and a wondrous testimony as He returned to His people, of the fact that His hand was not shortened that He could not save. It reminds us of that time in the history of Israel's apostasy when the prophet Elijah issued his challenge in behalf of God to the prophets of Baal, with all the people as witnesses. It was to be no ordinary test. They were to see whether it was God or whether it was Baal. So the priests of Baal are allowed to take their sacrifices and, without unusual care, to see if they can bring down fire from heaven. When they had consumed the day in their vain cries and cutting themselves, and there was no response, and abashed and silent they had to wait for the voice of God, then it was that the prophet took those special precautions to manifest that it was indeed God and He alone who was dealing with His people. Water is again and again poured over the sacrifice, over the altar, until it fills the ditch about the altar, and when every possibility of fire has been removed, all nature's heat quenched, then it is that in a few simple words the prophet asks the Lord to manifest Himself. Ah, yes, He can do so now. He cannot manifest Himself where there are still smoldering embers of nature's efforts; and it is well for the sinner to realize this. The fire to be kindled by divine love comes from God, is not found in his heart. It would only be a denial of man's need of God. Nor must the saint forget the same truth.

And so the kine with their precious burden go on their way, unwilling enough as far as nature is concerned, lowing for their absent calves as they went, but not for a moment turning aside; and the lords of the Philistines who follow them are constrained at last to admit that God has vindicated His honor and manifested the reality of His own presence and His own care for His throne. They follow and see the ark deposited upon a great rock, may we not say, type of that unchanging Rock on which rests the throne of God, the basis of all sacrifice and of all relationship with Him, even Christ Himself? And here we leave the Philistines, who return to their home, glad, no doubt, to be well rid both of the plagues and of Him who had inflicted them.[1]

The ark returns to Beth-shemesh, "the house of the sun," for it is ever light where God manifests Himself, and His return makes the night indeed bright about us. It comes into the field of Joshua, "Jehovah the Savior," a reminder to the people whence their salvation alone could come. In vain would it be looked for from the hills, Jehovah alone must save. And here the spiritual instinct of the people, weak and ignorant as they are, is shown. They take the cattle and the wood of the cart and offer up a burnt-offering, far more acceptable to God than the golden images sent by the Philistines, of

---

[1] May we not reasonably think that this history of the ark and its deeds amongst the Philistines remained a powerful testimony among them, producing its fruits as we see in 2 Samuel 15:18, where we find that Ittai and several hundred with him from Gath were following David?

which we hear nothing again.

But the lesson of God's honor has not been fully learned, and, alas! His own people must now prove that His ways are ever equal. If He is holy in the temple of Dagon, so that the idol must fall prostrate before Him; if that same holiness will smite the godless Philistine nation, it is none the less intense when it comes to His own people. In fact, as we well know, judgment will begin at the house of God, and as the prophet reminds the people that they only as a nation had been known of God, so far from this entitling them to immunity from punishment, it was the pledge that they would get it if needed: "Therefore will I punish you for your iniquities."

The men of Beth-shemesh rejoiced to see the ark, but they little realized the cause of its removal into the enemy's country, and the need of fear and trembling as they approached God's holy presence. They lift up the cover and look within the ark, and God smites of the people, and there is a great slaughter. It seemed a very simple thing to do. We may hardly say that it was an idle curiosity to see what was therein. Possibly they may have thought that the Philistines had taken away the tables of the covenant, or at any rate they would see what was there. Was it not the covenant under which they had been brought into the land? Was it not the law which had been given on mount Sinai, written with the very finger of God, and were they not as the people of God entitled to look upon these tables of stone? Ah, they had forgotten two things, that when Moses brought the first tables of stone down from the mountain, and saw the idolatry of the people dancing about the golden calf, he cast the stones out of his hand and broke them at the foot of the mountain. He would not dare either to dishonor the law of God by bringing it into a godless camp, or insure the destruction of the people by allowing the majesty of the law to act unhindered in judgment upon them for their sin. They also forgot the divine covering over those tables of stone, that golden mercy-seat, that propitiatory with its cherubim at either end, beaten out of pure gold, one piece, speaking of the righteousness and judgment which are the foundation of God's throne and which must ever be vindicated or He cannot abide amongst His people. So upon that golden mercy-seat the blood of atonement had yearly been sprinkled, the witness that righteousness and judgment had been fully vindicated in the sacrifice of a substitute, and that the witness of atonement was there before God as the ground upon which His throne could remain in the midst of a sinful people.

To lift off the mercy-seat was in fact to deny the atonement. To gaze upon the tables of the covenant was practically to lay themselves open to the unhindered action of that law which says: "Cursed is he that continueth not in all things that are written in the book of the law to do them." The law acted, we may say, unhindered, as the covering was removed.

How we should bless our God that His throne rests on the golden mercy-seat; that the blood of the Sacrifice has met every claim of a broken law, and faith delights to look where the cherubim's gaze is also fixed, upon that which speaks of a Sacrifice better than that of Abel—calling not for vengeance, but calling for the outflow of God's love and grace toward the guilty. Ah, no; God forbid that we should ever in thought lift the mercy-seat from the ark.

And so at last the lesson of divine holiness is in some measure learned. The people are forced, by the smiting of God, even though but just returned amongst them, to acknowledge that He must be approached with reverence and godly fear. "Who is able to stand before this holy Lord God?" Here unbelief struggles with reverence, and for the time triumphs; and instead of turning in simplicity to the One who had smitten them, to learn why, and how they could approach Him and enjoy His favor without danger, they are more concerned, as the Philistines had been, that the ark should go up from them, not of course to be taken out of their land, but still to be removed from their immediate presence—so that they could have the benefit of God's favor without the dread sense of His too near presence, a thing, alas, too common amongst God's professed people. And may we not detect in our own hearts a kindred feeling which would shrink from the constant sense of the presence of God in every thought and word and act of our lives, and would rather have Him, as it were, at a little distance, where we can resort in time of need or as desire may move us, but where we are not always under His eye? Thank God, it is vain to wish this, it cannot be; and yet as to our experience, how often are we losers in our souls because the desire of the psalmist is not more completely our own: "One thing have I desired of the Lord, that will I seek after, that I may dwell in the house of the Lord, and inquire in His temple."

And so the ark cannot yet find a resting-place in the midst of the nation, but is sent off to Kirjath-Jearim, "the city of the woods;" strange contradiction, and suggestive of the place of practical banishment into which God was being put, a city in name and yet a forest. Here David finds it (Psalm 132:6). "We found it in the fields of the wood;" no place, surely, for the throne of God; yet here it abides for twenty years (1 Samuel 7:2), until the needed work of repentance is fulfilled. We can well believe them to have been years of faithful ministry on the part of Samuel, and of gradual, perhaps unwilling submission and longing, on the part of the people. We are told all the house of Israel lamented after the Lord. Meanwhile, the ark rests in the house of Abinadab in the hill, and his son Eleazar, with the priestly name "my God is help," remains in charge.

The ark never again returns to Shiloh: "He forsook the tabernacle of Shiloh, the tent which He placed among men, and delivered His strength into captivity and His glory into the enemy's hand" (Psalm 78:60-61). "He refused the tabernacle of Joseph and chose not the tribe of Ephraim" (Psalm 78:67). "Go ye now unto My place which was in Shiloh, where I set My name in the first and see what I did to it for the wickedness of My people Israel" (Jeremiah 7:12).

There was fitness in this in two ways. God never restores in exactly the same way a failed testimony. Shiloh had, as it were, become defiled and its name connected with the apostasy of the people under Eli. It had the dishonor of having allowed the throne of God to be removed into the enemy's hands. It had, so to speak, as the representative of the nation, proven its incompetency to guard

God's honor, and it could not again be entrusted with it.

Then, too, it was in the tribe of Ephraim—that tribe which spoke of the fruits of the life in contrast to Judah, from which tribe our Lord came, and whose name, "praise," suggests that in which alone God can dwell: "Thou inhabitest the praises of Israel." Praise for Christ is the only atmosphere in which God can abide. How everything emphasizes the refusal of the flesh! Even as Joseph himself displaced Reuben the first-born, and as Ephraim, the younger brother, was chosen before Manasseh, so now again the tribe which had had the headship and out of which the nation's great leader, Joshua, had come, must be set aside. "The Lion of the tribe of Judah" is the only One who can prevail, and all these changes emphasize this fact which God has written all over His word—there is no reliance in man, the flesh is unprofitable, Christ is all.

CHAPTER 4
GOD'S MERCY TO HIS HUMBLED PEOPLE

1 Samuel 7

At last the faithful ministry of Samuel was about to produce manifest fruit. The twenty years of humbling had gradually, no doubt, led the people to an increasing sense of their own helplessness, of their absolute dependence upon God and a glimmer, at least, of that holiness without which He could never manifest Himself on their behalf. So Samuel now can say to them: "If ye do return unto the Lord with all your hearts, then put away the strange gods and Ashtaroth from among you, and prepare your hearts unto the Lord and serve Him only and He will deliver you out of the hand of the Philistines." This searching of heart had prepared them to receive this word now. Their return to the Lord, gradual though it may have been, was now sincere and had that measure of whole-heartedness which His grace is ever ready to recognize. He cannot endure a feigned obedience, and yet with the best of our repenting there is ever mingled something of the flesh. How good it is to remember that if there be a real turning, He recognizes that, and not the imperfection that accompanies it!

But a true turning to Him is of an intensely practical character and is shown in the life. If He has His place in the heart or in the land, all strange gods must be put away. All the loathsome idolatry, copied from their neighbors, must be judged, and God alone have His place. He cannot endure a heart divided between Himself and a false god. While all this is perfectly simple, yet there must be preparation and purpose of heart if it is to be carried out effectually and permanently. To serve Him alone means how much for ourselves; how much more indeed than for Israel, whose service was to a great extent of an outward character, at least so far as the nation was concerned. If they are ready for this, then there is the distinct promise: "He will deliver you out of the hand of the Philistines." God Himself had removed His ark from the Philistines' land, yet, until the people were in a true state before Him, He could not in His holiness rescue them from the power of the same enemy.

Through God's mercy, Israel acts and the land is cleansed under the power of the ministry of Samuel whose life we have traced from its beginning. No longer now a child, in the full maturity of his powers he is in a position to be used, not now in a limited circle, but for all Israel. As his word had brought them to repentance, he now turns in intercession to God: "Gather all Israel to Mizpah and I will pray for you unto the Lord." The man who speaks for God to the people is the one who is able to speak to God for the people. The man in whom the word of God abides and who is faithful in using it will know much, too, of the priestly privilege of intercession, while those who may have as clear a view of the evil, but dwell upon that merely without divine power, are never brought into God's presence about it, and so are themselves overwhelmed by it rather, and rendered helpless instead of being prevailing intercessors.

We may well remark, in passing, upon the importance of being occupied with evil only to deal with it according to the word of God, and thus to be able to work a deliverance through His word and intercession with Him. There is always hope, even in a day of decline and ruin, when there are intercessors amongst the people of God; those who, if they know nothing else to do, at least know where to turn for help. Private intercession often opens the way to more public ministry, and this in turn to fresh prayer for God's recovering grace.

And so the people are gathered together to Mizpah. Common needs, common danger, and above all, a common turning to God will bring His people together. All other gatherings are worthless and worse. Here they pour out water before the Lord and fast and acknowledge their sin afresh. The pouring out of water and fasting seem to be but two sides of the same act, expressed probably in the words which follow: "We have sinned against the Lord." The pouring out of water seems to be an acknowledgment of their utter helplessness and worthlessness. "We are as water spilled upon the ground which cannot be gathered up again." They had spent their strength for naught and were indeed as weak as water. This weakness had come from their sinning against God. So it is proper that fasting should accompany this solemn act, no mere religious form or unwilling abstinence from food, as though there were some merit in that, but that intense earnestness of spirit which is so absorbed in its purpose that necessary food is for the time forgotten, or refused as an intrusion upon the more important business before the soul. Fasting, as a means to produce certain desired effects, savors too much of ritualism and fosters self-righteousness in its devotees but as a result—as an indication of the state of soul—it is always the mark of a truly earnest seeker after God.

A people thus self-judged, and in humiliation before Him, are now in position to receive with profit the ministry of God's truth; so Samuel can now judge them, take up in detail their walk, ways and associations, and deepen that work which God had already begun in their souls. It is not enough to say in a general way: "We have sinned against the Lord." This, if real, includes all else, but for that very reason, details can then be gone into. A mere general judgment of self is too often but vague, and beneath its broad generalities may be hidden many a specific evil which has not been dragged out into the light, and judged according to God's holy word. Yet the two must come in this way: there must first be the judgment of ourselves, that state of true humility which is ready to bow before God, before there can be a helpful taking up of specific acts and testing them by the Word.

It is to be feared that we often fail in this individually, and in our efforts to help the saints of God. Unless one is truly humbled before God, truly broken, it is vain to reach a real judgment of specific wrong. Thus a trespass committed against a brother will be condoned, or that brother's own share in wrong doing will be brought up—an effectual check in true judgment of the act in question. What is needed is to get before God, to pour out before Him the water of a true and real judgment of ourselves according to His word—owning that we are capable of anything, yea, of everything, unless hindered by His grace, owning too our sin. This will enable us to judge calmly and dispassionately as to the details of the actual trespass. Would to God that this were realized more amongst us! There would be more true recovery of those who have gone wrong, and a consequent greater victory over our spiritual foes.

Then, too, the judging of the people suggests not merely looking at their past conduct, but ordering their present walk. Any associations, practices, worship, that were not according to His mind and which had up to this time been ignored by the people, or which they were in no true state to form a proper judgment upon, all these things would now come into review. Practices and principles will be tested by God's truth, and so the walk be ordered aright. To be low in His presence, as we said before, is the only place where we can be truly judged. It is a place of humbling, but after all, how blessed to be there! It is the place of power as well, for God is there. Israel at Bochim may not have been an inspiriting sight to nature. The flesh always despises that which humbles it, but Bochim is where the messenger of God can meet His repentant people and hold out to them hopes of deliverance. Israel, we may say, at Mizpah were again at Bochim.

But we may be sure that the enemy will never permit any recovery to God without making some special effort to hinder it. So, when the Philistines hear of this gathering of Israel, they go up against them. Are they not their slaves? Can they allow that which, while a manifestation of weakness, may lead to something else? And so with our spiritual foes. Satan will not object to the people of God dwelling upon evil and being so filled with it that they lose all power to judge it; but there is one thing that he always resists with all his energy and cunning, and that is a gathering together before God for humiliation and prayer. He abhors this. Formalism abhors it. Philistinism in all its

41

forms dreads seeing the people of God humbled in His presence. This will explain why the hour of prayer and searching of heart before God is so often interrupted by the intrusion of things which distract and hinder the soul. How often have we found individually, and unitedly too, that there were special difficulties in the way of getting low before God! This is the Philistine hindrance to God's work amongst us. Various reasons will often be given. It will be said that there is no hope, on the one hand, or no need on the other, of such an exhibition; that we had better be getting to work rather than humbling ourselves and doing nothing. This is ever a Philistine device to hinder a return to God and deliverance from formalism. Let us be on our guard; and as the apostle could say, "We are not ignorant of his devices," let us not be so easily duped by the wiles of the adversary.

The children of Israel are terrified at this array of the enemy. Their old masters are still that to them, and with consciences that remind them of their own unworthiness and failures, they do not seem to have the faith to lay hold upon God in face of the enemy; and yet there is a holding to Him, feeble though it be. They realize the need and the value of prayer. So they say to Samuel: "Cease not to cry to the Lord our God for us that He will save us out of the hand of the Philistines." They had indeed turned to Him, and though it is but a child's feeble cry of weakness, what child ever cried to a mother without moving her heart? What child, failing and weak and unworthy though he may be, ever cried to God without getting an answer? There had been a time when they would save themselves out of the hand of the Philistines. That has passed. The humbling lesson had been learnt. They have turned now to Him from whom alone their help can come, and not even the ark (that badge of His throne), but divine power itself in the midst of a self-judged people is their only hope.

There is more yet; for Samuel, nearest to God and therefore knowing His mind, not merely intercedes, but "took a sucking lamb and offered it as a burnt-offering wholly unto the Lord." Well he knew that the one way of approach, the only ground of merit, was sacrifice; and though himself not the priest, yet here in the place of the priest, he offers the burnt-offering to God, on the ground of which he can add his prayers. This lamb, of course, speaks to us of that "Lamb of God which taketh away the sin of the world," though here not as the sin-offering, but as the burnt-offering—Christ in His devotedness to God unto death, the Lamb without blemish or spot, whose life had proved Him personally well-pleasing and acceptable to God, and therefore whose death could be a Substitute for the disobedience and sin of His people.

Thus they have had, we might say, a threefold ministry. The Word has searched their hearts and brought them to repentance. The priestly intercession and sacrifice of Samuel have opened the way for God's power to be manifested, and, as judge, Samuel has taken the place of leader amongst the people. In all this, he no doubt foreshadows what Christ is in perfection for His people, the One who has brought home to our hearts the word of God by His Spirit, whose one sacrifice and all-availing intercession as our High Priest ever speak for us to God, and who as Leader carries us on to victory —the Prophet, Priest, and King.

Now let the Philistines draw near if they dare. They are meeting no more a boastful people, whether strong or weak. Their controversy is now not with Israel, but with Israel's God, and therefore the mighty thunder of the Lord is the answer to their proud assault. They are discomfited and smitten before Israel, and now the victory becomes a rout; the Philistines are pursued from Mizpah and all the way to Ebenezer. How significant that place becomes to them—not of previous defeat (1 Samuel 6:1), but giving its own meaning now, "hitherto hath the Lord helped us." Have we not known something of this? And what a joy it is to be able to triumph in our God in the very face of those enemies which once have been our masters and to whom, hopeless, we had rendered, even though unwilling, yet a servile obedience!

The victory is complete and lasting; the enemy came no more into the land all the days of Samuel's faithful ministry. But what hindered this from becoming an abiding permanence?—for there was subsequent bondage to these very enemies. The simple answer must be, no leader like Samuel, and no bowing to his judgment like that at Mizpah. It is important to notice that this deliverance under Samuel was not of a temporary or partial nature, it was no make-shift; though other lessons, with other sins and weaknesses amongst the people brought out the need of fresh deliverers. The great, all-prevailing truth had to be learnt in fresh ways, and that which was only partial or external in Israel had to be manifested—else Samuel was indeed another Moses, under whose rule, as type of Christ, the people might have gone on happily, recognizing none but God as their Ruler, and their guide him who spoke for God.

It is comforting, too, to see the recovery that takes place. Cities which had long been under Philistine sway, now that their power is broken over the nation, are restored. Peace follows as a result. So for us. If we in any way repeat the experience of Israel at Mizpah, there will be not merely a deliverance from present foes, but a restoration of many of those blessings, much of that spiritual truth which we have felt and enjoyed practically. "Cities to dwell in" will be restored to us and our coasts will be enlarged.

We now see the government of Samuel after the enemy has been thrust out of the land. He judges Israel all the days of his life. What a beautiful life it is; begun, we may say, in the heart of his mother before his birth—a man dedicated to God and His service; who in childhood heard His voice and obeyed it; who, as he grew, became more and more the suited instrument as the messenger for God; the first of the prophets—of that long line of spiritual and faithful witnesses who, during all the years of Israel's darkness and apostasy, yea, even of captivity, witnessed for Him, sought to bring back an alienated people, or failing in this, turned their gaze to Him who should come, the true Prophet, as the true King, and restore peace and blessing to the nation. But what a privilege to be a Samuel in dark days like these! May we not covet it for ourselves in our measure and station?

We have seen the special scene of judgment at Mizpah, but this was to continue, a thing that we often lose sight of. There must not merely be one act of self-judgment, but our whole lives are to come under the light of God's truth. The practical Word is to be applied to our ways. Samuel had four places in his circuit where he went from year to year to judge Israel; Bethel, Gilgal, Mizpah, and Ramah where his home was. There surely must be instruction in these names and the associations connected with them. They are well known in Israel's history.

Bethel is "the house of God;" all judgment must begin there. There is no power for judgment until we are in His holy presence. Judgment must begin, too, at the house of God, for holiness becometh that house forever. Here it was where God revealed Himself to Jacob at the first; and here, when he had forgotten, for his family, that holy separation which should ever mark the home of the saint, he was bidden to return: "Arise and go up to Bethel and dwell there."

The next place was Gilgal, the place of the rolling away of the reproach of Egypt. Here Israel had encamped on passing Jordan and coming into the land. As soon as they put their foot upon their heritage, they had to make themselves sharp knives for circumcision, and thus to roll away the reproach of Egypt, the badge of the world which was upon them. So for us, Gilgal follows Bethel. This world is judged and its reproach rolled away. Circumcision is practically made with the sharp knife of divine truth. The sentence of death is remembered afresh, and what the cross means for self. Here is the place of power indeed. Here we lay aside the livery of the world and shake off its yoke. We are now God's freemen, ready to do battle for all that He has given us in our goodly inheritance.

Next comes Mizpah, "the watch-tower." There has been that sense of God's presence suggested by Bethel, that judging of self at Gilgal where we have learnt, as the true circumcision, to have no confidence in the flesh; but how prone we are to forget, how easily do we glide back into the world, and need to be afresh reminded of what we thought we should never forget! The watch-tower, then, is needed to watch against the wiles of the enemy, to guard against that declension to which we are so prone. The very fact of our having been at Gilgal implies a danger of our getting away from it, or losing its holy lesson. We need to be on our guard. Many a saint has fallen because he forgot this obvious lesson and failed to meet the divine Judge at Mizpah. Let us watch and be sober.

Lastly he returns to Ramah, "the height," which suggests that exalted place on high of our true Judge, the Lord Jesus, where His home is. He has gone on high. He would lead His people there. "If ye be risen with Christ, seek those things which are above, where Christ is;" and so, as His abiding place is there, we are to learn to abide in our hearts there also. We are to let the light of that heavenly position where Christ is, and where we are, in Him, judge our "members which are upon the earth," and which we can thus mortify (Colossians 3). The circuit of judgment is not complete until this heavenly character has been stamped upon it. It is, of course, very similar to Bethel, but there the thought is simply the presence of God. Ramah suggests, in its height, that heavenly character which should mark His people: "Our citizenship is in heaven."

Beloved, shall we not crave for one another the the benefit of this fourfold judgment? This sense of the presence of God in His own holiness; this judging and refusing of self; this sober, careful, humble watching, and the separate, heavenly character which comes from entering fully into the fact that Christ is not in the world nor of it, and so neither are we of the world. Here is the place of worship. Here Samuel dwelt, and here it is our privilege to dwell and share, with an exalted Christ, in the sweet savor of that sacrificial altar upon which He offered Himself a sacrifice for a sweet smelling savor unto God. In the value of that sacrifice, Israel was safe, shielded from her enemies. So are we.

CHAPTER 5
THE PEOPLE'S DESIRE FOR A KING

1 Samuel 8

In a world where death reigns, all things, even the good, must come to an end. Samuel grows old. His well-spent life is reaching its close. It is then that he makes the first mistake which is recorded of him; a natural mistake indeed, and yet evidently he had not the mind of God in what he did. He makes his sons judges at Beersheba. Here we have in essence the whole principle of natural succession recognized. Because the father was a judge, the sons must be judges. It reminds us of that plea of Abimelech, the son of Gideon: "My father [was] king," which suggests the succession from father to son, of office. The name Abimelech was a Philistine one given to their kings, as the title Pharaoh to those of Egypt, and it is really nature's substitute for dependence upon God. It is sad and strange to think of the victor over the Philistines falling into one of the snares peculiar to that people. A carnal and formal religion is based upon the principle of succession. "No bishop, no church" conveys a certain truth if it is man's church that is in question. It is through the bishops that succession comes—remove that, and the whole fabric of Rome and sacerdotalism generally would fall to the ground.

Gideon had refused absolutely this principle, even for himself or his descendants. He had left the power with Him who had given it, God Himself: "I will not rule over you, neither shall my son rule over you. The Lord shall rule over you" (Judges 8:23). So, too, Moses, when told that he could not lead Israel any further than the border of the land, and that he must lay down his leadership, did not presume to name his successor, much less to think of his own son as taking up that which he had laid down. How beautiful it is to see this meekness in the great leader, who, we may well suppose, as he felt so keenly the deprivation, would have loved to temper it by the privilege of naming his successor. But self is obliterated, and nowhere does his character show more beautifully than: "Let the Lord, the God of the spirits of all flesh, set a man over the congregation who may go out before them, and who may go in before them, and who may lead them out, and who may bring them in, that the congregation of the Lord be not as sheep which have no shepherd. And the Lord said unto Moses, Take thee Joshua, the son of Nun, a man in whom is the Spirit…And Moses did as the Lord commanded him" (Numbers 27:16-22).

In this way Joshua is as directly called of Jehovah as Moses himself had been. Unquestionably he was fitted by his own association with Israel's leader to carry on the work which he laid down, and it is equally probable that Moses himself might have chosen Joshua as his successor, but the point is that he did not do so; he left it entirely to God, realizing that wisdom and power for such responsibility could not be conferred by the hands of man, but must come from Him alone in whom all power is.

Without unduly criticizing the honored and faithful prophet of whom we are speaking, Samuel seems to have failed to see the immense importance of this. There is no mention of any turning to God and asking that He would select a successor. He seemed to forget the history of the judges, when, for each emergency, God Himself had raised up the judge of His own choice to deliver His people. He would do it himself. His decision is accepted by the people. No question is raised, no opposition apparently is made, but God was not in it, and so the sons show what they are. They take bribes and pervert judgment, and, instead of perpetuating the honor of God as their father had done, they indirectly bring reproach upon him, subjecting him to the humiliation of a public rebuke by the people, and weaken in their minds that faith in God's sufficiency which it had been Samuel's great effort to establish.

Nor is it necessary to suppose that these sons of Samuel were specially evil men. While reminded of them, we cannot class them with the apostates, Hophni and Phinehas, whose wickedness was of such a gross and glaring character as to bring down the immediate judgment of God. It is to be noted that they failed as judges, their wrong-doing confined to the exercise of that office into which they had been intruded. They took bribes and perverted judgment. Lord Bacon, whose wisdom and greatness, and, we would fain hope, his Christianity, are beyond dispute, failed in the same way. He was officially disgraced, and yet even in his own time his personal character and abilities were recognized to a certain extent. It was felt that the man was better than the officer, and that his position was responsible for bringing out that inherent weakness of moral character which might have remained in abeyance had he not been unduly tempted. At any rate, we may well conceive that Samuel's sons in other respects were fairly blameless men, and had they been allowed to continue in private life or in the path to which God Himself would have called them, might never have fallen into the sin which is the only record that we have of their lives.

All this emphasizes the importance of what we have been dwelling upon. God will never delegate to the hands of man responsibility for transmitting that which comes alone from Himself. The failure to see this has been one of the fruitful causes of all the apostasy of the professing Church from the earliest times. Man desires to have things in his own hands, and, having them there, only proves how utterly incompetent he is to administer these great and solemn responsibilities. So the ordination of men to office but fixes the man in a position which may not be of God at all. If a man has been divinely called, he needs no human authorization and, if not called, all such authorization is but confirming a human mistake, and paving the way for such failure as we see in Samuel's sons. This touches upon a most profound and far-reaching subject. The leaven of Samuel's mistake has permeated all Christendom until it seems heresy to dispute the principle of succession, and yet is it not a distinct denial of the presence and sufficiency of the Holy Spirit, who dwells in the Church to guide, control and actuate all ministry?

Returning to Samuel's mistake in thus making his sons his successors, we are led to ask how far it showed his failure to bring up his children aright. Had he unconsciously imitated the weakness of Eli, with whom he was associated in early life, and whose family failure was of such a glaring character as to be the cause of God's sorest judgments? It would hardly seem likely, for he had warning before his eyes and from the lips of God Himself. He himself in his childhood had been the messenger to unfaithful Eli as to this very matter, and he witnessed the captivity of the ark, the death of Eli's sons, and of the high priest himself, all because of this indifference. His own personal faithfulness with the people at large, his prayerfulness, forbid the thought that he was careless or indifferent as to his responsibility in his own home. On the other hand, are we not reminded in Abraham, that he would "command his household after him," and in Joshua's strong words, "As for me and my house we will serve the Lord," that they link the family together with the father? Are we not told in the New Testament that one indispensable requisite for a leader of the people of God is that he should "rule well his own house"? Carelessness in the home would mean carelessness everywhere else, or a foolish and undue severity in just the place where it was not called for, as Eli could rebuke poor Hannah at her prayer, while his sons reveled in godlessness unrestrained.

May the truth not lie between these two extremes? That Samuel was not entirely without blame we have already seen. He failed to grasp the mind of God. We may well believe that his frequent absences from home, the absorbing interest in a nation at large, unconsciously to himself closed his eyes to responsibilities at home which no weight of public care could relieve him of. "Mine own vineyard have I not kept" has only too often had to be the sorrowful confession of those who have labored in others' vineyards. It is not a thing to excuse nor explain away, but solemnly to face and to remember the danger for us all, if such a man as Samuel, with such an example as that of Eli before him, could in any measure commit a similar wrong. May God's mercy be upon the heads of families, giving grace and dependence and prayerfulness that the households may be an example of submission to His order!

These sons were, after all, but a reflection of the state of the entire people, and even of the flesh in Samuel himself, and so in man generally. Wherever mere nature acts, we may be sure it does not act for God. Hence even natural affection, the strong ties that bind the household together, if not controlled by the word of God and the Holy Spirit, may do the very opposite of His will. How different from Levi, "who said unto his father and to his mother, I have not seen him; neither did he acknowledge his brethren, nor knew his own children: for they have observed Thy word, and kept Thy covenant" (Deuteronomy 33:9). Therefore they would be qualified for wider service: "They shall teach Jacob Thy judgments and Israel Thy law" (verse 10). How perfect in this, as in all else, was our blessed Lord Jesus, who rendered all due obedience in its place, and whose words from the cross itself bespoke a tender love and care for His mother; and yet, whenever nature intruded between Himself and His Father's will, how He could rebuke her, or show that obedience to God was to Him a clearer proof of relationship than any mere natural tie! "Whosoever shall do the will of God, the same is my brother and sister and mother."

Was it not, also, a certain measure of unbelief in Samuel in the sufficiency of God and care for His own beloved people that led him to appoint successors? We cannot therefore be surprised when the contagion of this unbelief spreads to the people at large; and so they come to Samuel as seeing the very thing which he himself had seen, and desiring to provide against it in much the same way in which he had attempted to do: "Behold, thou art old, and thy sons walk not in thy ways; now make us a king to judge us, like all the nations." Was it not, after all, simply seeking to remedy a manifest evil, which was all too plain, by recourse to a human expedient rather than to God Himself?

In passing, we may notice the humiliation to which Samuel was subjected in thus having to hear from the lips of those whom he himself had judged, sad words in relation to the failure in his own family: "Thy sons walk not in thy ways." Alas, too true, and we can well conceive the shame that would mount to the aged prophet's cheeks as there, before the people, the sad state of his own house was declared to him! There is no mention of any resentment, and, from all we know of this dear and honored servant's faithfulness to God, we may well believe that he bowed under what would seem most clearly to have been a chastening from God's hand. We never gain by refusing such chastenings, painful and humbling though they may be. Let us be more concerned to avoid the cause of them, the need for them, than the shame of being subjected to them. May God write this lesson deeply in our hearts!

"Like all the nations." How human this is! It is as though they were like all the nations. It is putting themselves on the same plane with those very Philistines whom but lately they had overthrown in the power of God alone. Alas, so easily do we forget and so quickly turn away from our blessed God, who would have us different from all the nations! Had He not singled them out as a peculiar people in His electing choice, by the wondrous signs in the land of Egypt, by the sheltering blood, and bringing them forth with a high hand and an outstretched arm? Had He not guarded them as the apple of His eye all through "that great and terrible wilderness"? Had He not cast out the nations from the land of Canaan and given them an inheritance—houses which they had not builded and vineyards which they had not planted? What nation had ever been so treated? This wretched word "like all the nations" is a denial in one breath of their whole history. If they were to be like all the nations, they would be still among the flesh-pots of Egypt, groaning in bitter and hopeless bondage.

And for ourselves, does not the desire for human remedies for recognized evils, for some resemblance to the ways of men about us, deny all that divine grace has done for us in making us a peculiar people for God Himself? Has not our salvation marked us out as distinct from the world in which we live? Has not the blood of the everlasting covenant forever separated between us and the judgment-doomed multitude who go on in their own way? Does not the presence of the Holy Spirit as a seal upon each of us mark us in God's eye, as it also should in the eye of the world, as "not of the world" even as Christ is not of the world? Do we desire to be "like all the nations"? No; in the name of all the grace and love of our God, of the all-sufficiency of His blessed Son, let us repudiate the faintest whisper of such a thought, and go on with acknowledged weakness, so feeble though it be as to be a subject of mockery to the world; let us as Jacob halt upon our thigh that the power of Christ may rest upon us, rather than seek for any human expedient like the world around us.

It is beautiful to see how Samuel turns in all this to God. His heart is grieved at what the people have asked, nor is there the slightest suggestion of the repetition of his previous failure, which stands out alone, and that by implication only, as we have seen, in a character otherwise unmarred by any manifest blemish. Samuel prayed unto the Lord. Well would it be for us, when we hear of weakness in others, to bring it before God and pour it out there, rather than seek weakly to reprove or correct it by our own efforts. He gets, in a certain sense, comfort from God and yet no relief in the ordinary sense of the word. He must hearken to the voice of the people in all that they say, and then the sad fact comes out that this had been the treatment to which the blessed God Himself had been subjected by this same nation from the beginning: "They have not rejected thee, but they have rejected Me, that I should not reign over them. According to all the works which they have done since the day that I brought them up out of Egypt, even unto this day, so do they also unto thee." Samuel must expect the same treatment from the nation as God Himself had received. The one who stands with God must feel what the psalmist felt: "The reproaches of those that reproached Thee are fallen upon me." Man's hatred of God was never more fully manifested than in the cross of our blessed Lord Jesus, and all that He was subjected to at the hands of man but manifested the treatment that they had in heart accorded God. Sad and sorrowfully true it is; and yet what an honor in any measure to be permitted to stand for God, even to suffer the reproaches, to meet with the treatment, which our blessed Lord met with: "If they have persecuted Me, they will persecute you also."

But the people are not allowed to have their own way without having a divine and perfectly clear warning as to where that way will lead, and so Samuel is instructed to tell them what it means to have a king, like the nations. In brief, they will be slaves to their king: "He will take your sons and appoint them for himself for his chariots, and to be his horsemen, and some shall run before his chariots." They will no longer be servants of God in that sense, and no longer free to labor for their own profit. They will be liable at any time to be called upon by their king to engage in war, needless or otherwise, as his fancy may dictate, to be menials about his house, to be servants of his servants.

Then, too, their property will not be safe from his aggression. Their lands can be taken away. The tenth part of their increase, the very same that Jehovah claimed as His own, must be given to their king. In other words, they would bitterly rue their choice, and find that from the perfect freedom of service to God they had passed into the bondage of human tyranny. How fully this was verified in after years, a glance at their history will show. Even David, in his awful sin, exemplified the arbitrary character of kingly power—a royal murderer, against whom no hand could be lifted in vengeance! Solomon's oppression, that of Asa, the glaring robbery and murder of Ahab, are but illustrations of what was, doubtless, but too common amongst the kings of Israel, who in turn were, no doubt, held in from going to the extremes of other nations by the restraining witness of the prophets constantly sent from God. From that time onward, royalty, if that in reality, has been but another name for self-will, oppression and tyranny, save where, in the mercy of

God, His grace overruled. It is not that a king necessarily must be a tyrant, but human nature being what it is, it is what is to be expected. God's thought, after all, is for a king, but it must be the true King, who shall reign in righteousness, of whom there is but One in all the universe of God. When He comes whose right it is to rule, and the government is upon His shoulders, oppression will cease, the meek shall be judged, and the oppressed shall be rescued, as is beautifully set before us in the seventy-second psalm.

Nor let it be thought for a moment that there is no necessity for human government at the present time. Kings and all that are in authority are, after all, but "the powers that be;" and the fault is not in the power, but in the men who misuse that power. But for a people who had God as their Ruler, for whom He had interposed in an especial way, it was nothing short of apostasy to desire a king like the nations. However, after the solemn witness is borne and the people repeat their desire, they are left—solemn thought—left to their choice. They shall have their request, even though it bring leanness to their own souls. Our blessed God often permits us to have our own way, that He may show us the folly of it. Alas, would that we might learn His way in His own presence, and be spared the sorrow for ourselves and the dishonor to His name which come from the bitter experience of a path of disobedience.

Again Samuel rehearses all the words of the people to the Lord, and again he is told to hearken to the voice of the people, who are for the time dismissed with the tacit promise that, as they have desired, so it shall be. Sad journey homeward, as every man goes to his own city after having deliberately refused longer to be under the mild and loving sway of the only One who could be truly their ruler!

PART TWO

CHAPTER 6
THE CALL OF THE KING

1 Samuel 9–10:16

The people having definitely decided to have a king, in face of all the warnings given by the prophet, nothing remains but to give them their desire according to the fullest thought of it. Had the choice of the ruler been left to a few, he would not have been really the expression of the people's wish. This difficulty is constantly encountered in the effort to secure a ruler who shall represent the desires of the people. The nearest that can be done is to let the majority decide. This at best but gives the preference of that majority, in which the rest of the nation has to acquiesce, and so man can never get the ideal ruler of his choice.

For Israel, God mercifully intervenes and, as we might say, puts at the disposal of the people His omniscience in selecting the ruler, not after His heart, but who He knows will meet their desires. This is an interesting and important point, one too that has a New Testament illustration, which, if understood, will throw light upon that which has been a difficulty for many.

The people had already turned against God and rejected Him from being their Ruler. Most certainly, then, their mind was not in accord with His. The king of their ideal would be a far different man from any whom God would Himself select. They had in their minds a ruler like those of the nations, whose first thought was the welfare of the people and the overthrow of their enemies. God's thought would be a man who first of all sought His glory, and was in subjection to Himself. We must remember that He is not choosing a king for Himself, but for the people. He does for them that which it would have been impossible for them to do for themselves, so that the result is exactly what they would have done had they been able.

The New Testament illustration of this is the selection of Judas Iscariot as an apostle. It has been said, did not the Lord know at the beginning that Judas was a traitor? We are distinctly told so in the sixth chapter of John, and may be certain that our blessed Lord was neither deceived nor disappointed—save in divine and holy sorrow over a lost soul—in the result. But this does not mean that our Lord put Judas in a position against his will or for which he was not in the judgment of men specially fitted. Judas himself had taken the place of a disciple. It was, therefore, simply selecting one who had already taken this place, and not imposing upon him a profession which he had not assumed for himself. Nay, more, the position of apostle was calculated to foster, if it existed at all, the faith of the disciple. The twelve were in the place of special privilege and nearness to the Lord, constantly under His influence, with His example before them as we know with much individual instruction according to the need of each. Who could associate with such a Master and witness His deeds of love, the flashing out of His holy soul, His tender heart of compassion, His sympathy, and not be made a better man if there were anything of grace in his soul at all? If Judas apostatized and the wickedness of his heart came out in face of all this, we may be sure it is only a special proof of the hopeless corruption of a heart that has not been visited by God's grace. At the same time our Lord would not be violating in the least the free agency of the man or compelling him into anything counter to his nature.

Returning now to the king of Israel's choice, we will see in what is before us how divine care and foresight gave the fullest expression to the desire of the people, so that the result was one upon whom all the desire of the nation was fixed. But while man's self-will was thus at work and his rejection of God's mild and loving authority showed the determined alienation of his heart from Him, on the other hand, God was working out His own counsels, and His purposes were being unfolded too. The thought of a king was in His heart as well as that of the people, but how different a king! Hannah had given expression to this divine desire for a Ruler for His people at the close of her song, which is fittingly so like that of Mary, the mother of the true King.

The main theme of that song (1 Samuel 2:1–10) is that God raises up the poor and the lowly, and overcomes all pride. Thus His enemies and those of His believing people are overthrown, and the needy and the afflicted are raised up. "He raiseth up the poor out of the dust and lifteth up the beggar from the dung-hill, to set them among princes and to make them inherit the throne of glory." Our blessed Lord laid aside all heaven's glory, and, so far as earthly greatness was concerned, associated Himself with the poor rather than those who occupied the throne. The throne, so far as it could any longer be called that, was occupied by a Herod, while back of him was the power of imperial Rome, the scepter having passed over to the Gentiles. The One "born King of the Jews" was to be found in a stable, and faith alone could recognize Him as the Man of God's choice. But faith does recognize Him, and Hannah looks forward not merely to him who was to be the type of Christ, but to the Lord's Anointed Himself. She closes her song with the triumphant strain: "He shall give strength unto His King, and exalt the horn of His Anointed."

Well did God know that there must be a ruler for His people. Everything had been temporary, even the giving of the law itself at Sinai. There could be no permanent relationship between a nation and God, save through a Mediator. The only ruler could be, not some human deliverer, type of Him to come, but One who truly delivered them from bondage worse than that of Pharaoh and from a captivity greater than any inflicted by the Canaanites. Thus Joshua, and Moses himself, were but types of Christ. The deliverer, too, must be priest as well as ruler, and from Aaron on, the high priests and their sacrifices were but shadows of that perfect Priest who offered up Himself to God. The King was to be also a Priest, and in one blessed

Person was to embody all that the righteousness and glory of God, on the one hand, and the need of sinful man, on the other, required.

> "All things that God or man could wish
> In Thee most richly meet."

So the very unbelief of the people, expressing a desire for a ruler, was but the occasion for God to approach one step nearer the accomplishment of His own purposes but He was not to be hurried into taking more than one step at a time. He does not—reverently we would say, He cannot give His own King yet. He must let them work out and manifest all the results of their own desires, and so far from impelling them into that which would show the worst side of self-will, He guards them in every way from this. Thus He uses divine wisdom to select the best man according to their judgment, offering every facility, the machinery of divine Providence, we might say, to secure such a man, and when he is chosen, not withholding all aid, encouragement and warning. If the king of their choice does not succeed, the blame can never be laid upon God. This will be fully manifest. And may we not say the same as to the natural man in every way? If he manifests his corruption, his enmity of God, his hopeless alienation from Him, it is not because of the circumstances in which he is placed, but in spite of them. The very world which has been given over to Satan is still full of witness of God's power, wisdom and goodness. Every man's life, with its history of mercies and of trials, is a witness that One is seeking to hide pride from him and to deliver him from his worst enemy—himself. The whole providential government of the world and its long continuance in its present state is a witness of the same. God gives man a free hand to work out all that is in his own heart, while at the same time surrounding him with every inducement to turn to Himself.

This is particularly true of the last phase of His patience and long-suffering—the present dispensation, where, in Christendom at least, the full blaze of revelation would guide and attract man into paths of pleasantness and peace. When all is over (and it seems now to be nearly the end) it will be seen that if there were anything good in man there had been just the atmosphere in which it would properly develop, and so far from God being an indifferent spectator, or a hostile one to human progress and development, it will be clear that He has done all that He could to make the trial a successful one on man's part. It will be true of Israel as a nation, and her kings and the world at large as well, that but one answer could be given the question: "What could I have done more unto My vineyard that I have not done?" All has been done.

Our chapter opens with the genealogy of king Saul. It is traced back through five ancestors, whose names are given, and the significance of which cannot fail to be suggestive. We must bear in mind that it is a genealogy of the flesh, as we may say, where that which is emphasized will be nature rather than grace. Saul himself means "asked" or "demanded." He represents the people's demand for a king, and in that way, nature's ideal. His father was Kish, which means "ensnaring," very suggestive of all that is of nature, which in its most attractive form cannot be trusted.

The next in line was Abiel, "father of might," which seems to emphasize the thought of strength in which man does indeed glory, but which too often proves to be utter weakness. Zeror, the next, "compressed" or "contracted," suggests the reverse; we can readily understand how one, himself hedged in and oppressed, would seek a reaction and give expression to his desire in his son. Bechorath, his father, "primogeniture," is that which nature makes much of and which Scripture has frequently set aside. Nature says the elder shall rule. How often has Scripture declared that the elder shall serve the younger! Aphiah, "I will utter," would suggest that pride of heart which tells out its imagined greatness. The last person in the list is not named, but described as a Benjamite, a member of that tribe whose history had been one of such glorying self-will and rebellion.

Thus the genealogy of the man of the people's desire would suggest the pride, the self-will, the excellence of nature, together with its feebleness, too, and its deceit. These things are not looked upon as man would regard them, where many of the traits are considered valuable and important, but they are looked upon from God's point of view, and all that is great and excellent in nature is seen to be stained with decay. Thus Saul is described as "a choice young man and a goodly, and there was not among the children of Israel a goodlier person than he. From his shoulders and upward he was higher than any of the people," surely a beau ideal of a king, in man's eyes; alas too soon to show the vanity of man's nature!

The man of the people's desire being now marked out, we are next shown the steps which lead up to his being presented. What trivial events apparently decide our whole after-course of life! It was comparatively an unimportant matter that the asses of Kish should have strayed away and Saul with a servant be sent in search of them, and yet God used this to bring to pass all that was hinging upon it. No doubt everything here has its lessons for us if we are able to read them aright. We are told that man is like a wild ass's colt, naturally unrestrained and self-willed. These asses would then naturally suggest that nature of man which has gone astray from God, and in its wildness and absence of restraint needs ever the strong hand to hold it down. Israel, too, had many a time shown its waywardness in like manner, and one who goes in search of that rebellious nation must indeed have help from God to lay hold of it.

As a matter of fact, Saul did not find the asses; they were restored to his father by divine Providence; and no mere man has ever brought back the wayward wanderer to God. If brought back at all, it is through a divine work. When the time comes for the true King to enter His city, He rides upon an ass's colt upon which man had never sat, controlling all things. Saul searched diligently enough in various places for these lost asses, but fails to find them. First he goes through Mount Ephraim, "fruitfulness," and the land of Shalishah, "the third part," which may have stood for a very large territory; but neither in the place of fruitfulness nor in any wide extent of region has a wanderer ever been found. Man surely has not been fruitful for

God. He next seeks through the land of Shaalim, "the place of hollows or valleys" and the land of Jemini, "my right hand," which would suggest exaltation. But neither in humiliation nor exaltation is the natural man found. The poor and degraded are as far from God as those who are exalted. Lastly he comes to Zuph, "a honey-comb," and there he gives up the search. It would seem to stand for the sweetness and attractiveness of nature, but perhaps more hopeless than any is this. One may be naturally attractive without one thought of God, and if the best have no heart for Him, the search must be abandoned. It would need a Seeker after another kind to find the wanderers, and He found them in a different place from those in which Saul ever sought. Going down in death and taking his place under judgment, there He found the wanderer.

Saul has given up the vain search for the asses of his father, and now proposes to his servant to return home. But this one, like a true servant, seems to have a knowledge far beyond that of the favored son of Kish. He informs Saul that the prophet Samuel is in that place, and advises that, instead of human energy or hopelessness, they should go and inquire of him. Saul evidently has had no thoughts of turning to God in this matter, and apparently no knowledge of His prophet, and now can only suggest, as human righteousness is ever prone to suggest, that some price is needed if they are to get aught from God's hand. How like the natural man this is! He must bring his present to God if he is to receive anything from Him, and he knows nothing of that liberal Giver whose delight it is to give freely to those who have nothing with which to buy.

The confession of poverty on the part of Saul makes possible the servant's offer of the fourth part of a shekel of silver, which reminds us of that half-shekel of the atonement money which every child of Israel had to pay. Thus, whatever may have been the thought in the mind of the servant, or whether the price was ever actually handed to the prophet, there is a partial suggestion here, at least, that all approach to God, all learning of His mind, must be on the basis of atonement.

An explanation is next introduced showing the use of the terms "seer" and "prophet." In former times it was the custom to speak of the man of God as a "seer,"—one who sees the future, or that which is not visible to the eyes of sense. In other words, the people were more occupied with the result of the prophet's ministry than with its Source. The later word "prophet" suggests the Source from which he received all his inspiration, which then flowed forth from him. This explanation in itself is in keeping with all the circumstances at which we have arrived, both in Saul himself (who surely was not troubled about his relation with God, or how the man of God would gain his information, but rather with the benefit which he might receive from this divine insight) and in the nation at large, of which he was the fitting representative.

So Saul and his servant approach the city where the man of God was. What momentous changes are to occur within those walls! Inquiring their way, they find the object of their search. Everything here, no doubt, is suggestive. They are obliged to ascend to the city. A moral elevation must be reached if they are to enter in any measure into the revelations that are about to be given. Everything of God is on a plane far above the thoughts of the natural man. They are guided by the young maidens who were coming forth to draw water from the well.

This is a familiar scene in every oriental city, and frequently referred to in Scripture. The well with its water is a figure of that Word, which is drawn out of the wells of salvation. The maidens would remind us of that weakness, lowliness and dependence which alone can draw from these wells of salvation. The future king is directed to the man of God by these feeble instruments, which reminds us that God delights to use the weak things. It was a little captive Hebrew maid who told her mistress of the prophet in Israel, by whom Naaman, the great Syrian general, could be cleansed of his leprosy. Wisdom, in the book of Proverbs, sends forth her maidens with the message of invitation to the feast which she has spread. Feebleness which is getting its refreshment and strength from the word of God can point the mightiest to that which alone can give guidance or peace.

It is very suggestive, too, that it is upon the occasion of a public feast and sacrifice that Israel's future king meets the prophet. This falls in with what we have already said as to the atonement money. The basis upon which God's mind can be known, and in connection with which the anointing oil is to be poured upon the king, must be that of sacrifice.

In passing, it is well to notice that the disordered state of the nation is manifest here. There is a "high place" where the sacrificial feast is spread. This was in direct contradiction to the will of God as expressed in the book of Deuteronomy, which provides that it was to be only in the place where Jehovah put His name that sacrifices were to be offered and feasts celebrated. But the glory of the God of Israel had departed from Shiloh, where He had placed His name at the beginning, and the ark was abiding in "the field of the woods." There was no recognized center. Israel might be mourning after the Lord, but the time was not yet ripe for the pointing out of the true center of gathering for His people; nor was Shiloh to be thought of, because that, once forsaken, was never again to be recognized as the central abode of the glory of Jehovah.

Thus the high place was, we might say, a sort of necessity brought in by the failure and disordered condition of the people at large. We will find, also, that it was frequently used in this way. There was one at Gibeon, where King Solomon, later on, had a revelation from God. Thus they were not necessarily connected with idolatry. As a matter of fact, they were at the beginning devoted to the true worship of God, and to a certain extent were places where He Himself in grace recognized the need and met with His people, though not according to the due order which He Himself had provided. Later on, however, when He had established His center, placed His name at Jerusalem, and the temple of His glory was there, the worship of the high places was in direct disobedience to His will, and necessarily, therefore, became more and more connected with the idolatry to which the people were ever prone.

Thus, in the history of the faithful kings, we find that these high places were destroyed in some cases, and their idolatrous worship abolished; in others that in spite of all the manifold efforts to do away with them, they still remained, apparently not for idolatry, but for independent worship of God.

There is food for suggestive thought here. There can be no question that God meets individual faith wherever it truly turns to Him; but He has provided in His Word and by His Spirit for a true Center of gathering for His people, a corporate recognition of Christ Himself and His name as all-sufficient, of the word of God as the absolute guide, and the ever-present Spirit as the competent One to control, order and direct in worship, testimony, ministry, discipline, and whatever other functions there may be, of His people. To ignore this divinely provided Center, and to turn to human thoughts, to select places and modes of worship which are not provided for in the word of God, is really to worship in the high places. There is no question that very much of this is done in all sincerity, and God, as we were saying, meets His people in grace according to the measure of their faith. But can we wonder that when the truth of the unity of the Church of Christ, the sufficiency of His name and Word, are known, to go on in independency and self-will is but to prepare the way for wide declension from God, and eventually to lead to that dishonor to God which in Christianity corresponds with the material idolatry of which we have been speaking in the history of Israel?

Returning to the feast and sacrifice of which we were speaking, everything has almost a patriarchal simplicity about it. The prophet is, as we might say, another Abraham, living in a later age. The people will not eat of their feast until he comes and bestows his blessing, which at least would indicate their sense of dependence upon God and their desire to receive the blessing which His servant would bestow. The invited guests who share with the prophet in his feast were those, evidently, whose position in the city qualified them for the enjoyment of this honor.

Having received the directions as to meeting the prophet, Saul and his servant go on and find Samuel just going up to the high place. Everything has evidently been ordered of God, even to the appointed moment at which the meeting should take place. There is no waiting on the part either of the prophet or of him who was seeking him.

Moreover, Samuel is not surprised at this meeting, for the day before, the Lord had forewarned him as to all that is to take place—the visit of the man of the tribe of Benjamin, whom it was His will to anoint over His people Israel, and who should be the one to lead them in victory against their oppressors, the Philistines. At this first mention of the object for which the king was to be anointed, it is very suggestive and pathetic to remember that Saul never really won great victories over these very enemies against whom he was appointed to lead the people. The nation was more or less in bondage to the Philistines during his entire reign, and he met his end in the final battle at Mount Gilboa with these very people. Into this we shall look further as we go on; but we can see thus at a glance how ineffectual is all human adaptation to the end designed by God. He had harkened to the cry of His people and looked upon them in their need, for which He provided according to their thoughts and desires, rather than according to His own knowledge of what would really deliver them.

Not only has the prophet thus been forewarned of the visit of Saul, but, as he now meets him, he is assured by the Lord that this is the man of whom He spoke. Thus there is no possibility of mistake, and unerringly is the prophet's hand guided to pour the oil upon the appointed head. We can well conceive the surprise of Saul, as he approaches the prophet with his question, to find that both he and his errand, and all else, are well known to the man of God. He is invited to join with Samuel in the feast, and promised on the morrow that he shall be sent on home after all that is in his heart has been made known to him. His mind is set at rest as to the asses for which he had vainly searched, and he is furthermore told of his father's anxiety at his prolonged absence.

We can well understand how this evidence of divine knowledge on the part of the prophet would solemnize the heart of Saul, and make him realize that he was having to do, not with man, but with the living God. This would prepare the way for the next word that Samuel has to say—the desire of Israel is toward him and his father's house; that is, as Saul well understood it, the people wished just such a man as himself for king. This does not necessarily mean that they had their eye upon him individually, but that he was the kind of man who would answer to the desire which they had already expressed.

We have in what is next, an apparent humility on the part of Saul, which if it had gone more deeply would doubtless have been more permanent. He declares that he is a Benjamite, belonging to the smallest of the tribes of Israel, and his family one of the least in that small tribe. He was doubtless familiar with the history of the tribe, and how it came to be reduced to such small proportions, because of the judgment inflicted upon it for the awful sin of Gibeah, and the shielding of those evil-doers. Had the tribe been properly exercised by this fearful chastisement, it would, as a whole, have been brought into a place of true humility before God, and have been prepared for exaltation. There is no indication, however, that there was any genuine self-judgment on the part of the tribe as a whole or any individuals in it, and their humility was rather compulsory than spontaneous.

This, it is evident, was also the case with Saul, from his subsequent history. He might speak in depreciation of his family and of his tribe, but as a matter of fact there is no evidence that there was the genuine judgment of self in the presence of God. It is one thing to have low thoughts of one's self as compared with one's fellows, but quite a different thing to take one's true place in the presence of divine holiness. The flesh knows how to be humble under stress of circumstances, but it knows nothing of that which judges its very existence, and compels it to be absolutely prostrate before God.

Saul is introduced, now, into the company of those who had been invited to the feast, and is given, in anticipation, the kingly place at the head of the table over all the invited guests. There is also set before him, at the command of the prophet, the special portion which had been reserved for the guest of honor; might we not say, Benjamin's portion for the leader of Benjamin's tribe? The shoulder was that part of the sacrifice of the peace offering which was eaten by the offerers. It was originally, as we see from the tenth of Leviticus, a part of the priest's portion, for himself and his family. Thus, Saul was admitted to the privileges of the priestly household: a very suggestive thought for one who needed priestly nearness if he were rightly to carry out the responsibilities which were suggested in the fact that the shoulder was set before him.

The sacrifice, as we well know, speaks of Christ as the One who, having made atonement for us, and who in His death was the Object of God's delight, is also the Food for His people's strength. In the peace offering there is a portion for the priest, for God, and for the offerer. Thus, the thought of communion, and the strength which flows from communion is the prominent one. The shoulder reminds us of Him of whom the prophet says: "The government shall be upon His shoulder." He only has strength to bear the responsibilities of rule, who first of all laid down His life in submission to the will of God and for the salvation of His people. Never will government be what it should be until this great fact is recognized and until the true King, who is also the true Priest and the true Sacrifice, takes up the burden upon His shoulders. But, in this sacrificial feast, we have at least an indication that is suggestive. If there is to be true qualification for government, it must be as one has assimilated the mind of Christ and has received from Him that strength for service which He alone can give.

Saul remains with Samuel that day, and when about to take his departure, early on the following day, is called by the prophet at daybreak—the beginning of a new day for Israel and for Saul—to the housetop, alone in isolation and elevation above all his surroundings. The prophet then accompanies him outside the city, and, the servant being sent on ahead, Samuel declares to him the purpose of God. The holy anointing oil is poured upon his head, and he receives the kiss of the prophet's benediction, perhaps in acknowledgement too of his allegiance to him. He is assured that the Lord has anointed him to be prince over His inheritance. This anointing with oil was a figure, of course, not only of the divine designation for a specific service, but of the qualification which accompanied that. The oil, as symbol of the Holy Spirit, would suggest the only power in which it was possible for him to carry out the responsibilities of that place into which he had now been inducted by the prophet speaking for God.

He is now ready to be sent away, but is told of three signs that will meet him that day and which will at once confirm him in the realization of the truth of all that has been done, and at the same time, no doubt, give suggestions as to his future path of service. These signs are not explained, which would suggest that Saul knew, at least, to whom he could turn for explanation, the Lord Himself. It was also to be supposed that one who realized that he was now having to do with God, would be suitably exercised by any such manifestations as are spoken of here.

The first sign was to be that, after leaving Samuel, he would find, by Rachel's sepulcher at the border of Benjamin, two men who would announce to him the finding of the asses and that his father's anxiety had been transferred from their loss to the prolonged absence of his son. Rachel's tomb was a type of Israel according to the flesh, and in a special sense, perhaps, of the tribe of Benjamin, the last son at whose birth his mother, Rachel, breathed her last. All these things would appeal to Saul in a special way. It would seem to emphasize for him the fact that if he were to be a true Benjamite, "the son of the right hand," he must enter into the fact that death must pass upon all the excellence of nature. It is by Rachel's sepulcher, at the grave of the old man, in refusal of all the excellence of mere nature, that faith is to learn its first lesson. If there is to be true service for God, it must be on the basis of the refusal of self. Here Saul was to learn that the asses were found; and, at the grave of self, one learns all the futility of his past activities. His father now yearns for him, which might well remind Saul that if he is at the grave of all that nature might count great, he is still the object of love; if a human love, how much more also of that love of God which finds its perfect display in the Cross which sets man aside, and there too, the channel for its unrestrained outflow toward us!

The next sign would emphasize the privileges of fellowship on the basis of redemption and worship. He passes on to the "Oak of Tabor." Rachel's sepulcher, as we have seen, speaks of the rejection and refusal of nature. Where one's natural strength is recognized as weakness, he is qualified to know whence true strength comes. Thus, the sepulcher is changed for the oak, which suggests might—the might of a new "purpose," as Tabor means. There he meets three men who are going up to Bethel, "the house of God," the place of communion and of divine sovereignty. They carry with them their offering, three kids, which reminds us of the sin-offering; and three loaves of bread, which speak of the person of Christ, communion; and a bottle of wine, of the precious blood of Christ and of the joy that flows from a knowledge of redemption through that blood. They would ask of his welfare. He would thus already receive at their hands the salutation which was now his kingly prerogative, and from them also he would receive the loaves of bread, which speak, as we have said, of Christ as the food for His people. Fitting reminder for a king—"royal dainties" truly.

Passing on further, he comes to the hill of God, and finds there not only the manifestation of divine presence, but the evidence of the enemy, too. There are outposts of the Philistines in the very place where God would manifest Himself. What a twofold suggestion to a newly made king that his work was to be, on the one hand, in the sanctuary of God's presence, and on the other, in facing the enemy who had intruded themselves there!

Here he would meet a company of prophets, men under the power of the Spirit of God and controlled by His Word; and, as he mingled with these, he too was to be changed from the man which he was, to come under the sway of that mighty, divine energy which controlled them. As we know from many Old Testament examples, it was, alas, possible for a person to come outwardly under the power of the Spirit, and even to be used as was Balaam to be the messenger of God's word, without any saving interest in His grace. There was this in this sign which was to meet Saul, and yet subsequent history shows that he was only an outward participant in this manifestation of divine power.

The prophets were not merely speaking under the power of God, but were accompanied by psaltery and harp; that is, there was the spirit of praise as as well of prophecy. In God's presence there is fulness of joy, and He dwelleth amidst the praises of His people. Thus worship should ever be an accompaniment of prophecy. Elisha, when called upon to ask counsel of God, called for a minstrel, in order that, as it were, his spirit might be fully attuned to the praise of God. We read also of prophesying with harps, where the spirit of praise gives the needed instruction to mind and heart. This would be a reminder to Saul that mere knowledge, even of a divine character, was never to be separated from that priestly worship and joy which cannot be simulated, but flow from a heart that is well acquainted with the grace of God, which alone can empower for true service and testimony.

Samuel had even told him that as he prophesied he would receive another heart. That is, there would be a change which would suggest permanency, while at the same time it left things open to the will of Saul himself. Surely, all that was to occur to him on that day, the testimony of the judging of the flesh at Rachel's sepulcher, of the sufficiency of Christ's atoning work and the presence of God in the second sign, and of the power of the Holy Spirit in the work of the prophets, would all tend to powerfully work upon heart and mind and conscience, so that if there were indeed life toward God, he would find here a complete revolution of his entire past.

The prophet then leaves him, as it were, to God. When all these signs came to pass, he could act under the guidance of God, for God was with him. At the same time, Samuel warns him to go on down to Gilgal and there to await his coming, where burnt-offerings and peace-offerings were to be offered up to God. He was to tarry there seven days, everything in complete abeyance, waiting for the coming of the prophet. This is most important in connection with what subsequently took place. Thus we see Saul, on the one hand, set free to act as God guided; and on the other, checked, and reminded that his place is at Gilgal, the place of self-judgment, of the refusal of all the excellence and glory of nature, of which the Israelite was reminded by that place.

How everything, in this whole history of the man after the flesh, emphasizes the fact that nothing of nature can glory before God. How everything was designed, as it were, to call Saul to judge and to refuse himself, in order that having no confidence in himself, he might be spared the terrible experiences and fall which marked his later history. It would seem as though God Himself were laboring to impress all these things upon the mind of the future king, and to spare him, so far as divine mercy could intervene, from the pride and self-righteousness which were the occasion of his final downfall and overthrow. May not we also need to learn well these lessons for our own souls, and have impressed more deeply upon us, as we grow more familiar with these facts, the necessity of having "no confidence in the flesh"?

All takes place as Samuel had predicted, and Saul seems fully to come under the control of the prophetic Spirit; but those who remembered what he was, asked, as if in mockery, (as they repeated the question in later years, under different circumstances) "Is Saul also amongst the prophets?" He had evidently not been characterized, up to that time, by any fear of God or faith in Him. It was a matter of astonishment that he should thus take his place with them. Alas, we know that it was but temporary. His uncle meets him too, with questions as to where he had been and what Samuel had told him, but here, in some Nazarite way, Saul keeps his counsel as to all that had been told him about the kingdom, and mentions to his uncle simply that which was external and which he had a right to know. This is good, so far as it goes, and was an indication of that spirit of reserve which to a certain extent characterized him in after years and which was, so far, a safeguard against feebleness.

CHAPTER 7
THE NEW KING

1 Samuel 10:17–11:15

God having dealt faithfully and fully with Saul in private and through the prophet, now manifests to the nation at large the man whom He has chosen for them. Samuel is again the honored instrument here and calls the people to meet the Lord, as he had already, so far as possible, brought the future king face to face with Jehovah. The people are to come together at Mizpah, the place where God had signally manifested His delivering hand in rescuing them from the Philistines, and also one of the stations where Samuel was accustomed to judge Israel. Its name, as we have seen, means "Watchtower," appropriate surely for those who would rightly survey the past and the future, and heed the admonitions with which God would address them. "I will stand upon my watch, and set me upon the tower and will watch to see what He will say unto me, and what I shall answer when I am reproved" (Habakkuk 2:1). Good would it have been, for them and their king, had this attitude of soul truly marked them. It was that indeed to which God called them, as He ever does His people, to hearken to the admonitions and reproofs of love, and thus to be guarded from the snares into which we will otherwise surely fall. Well would it have been for Peter had he been spiritually at Mizpah to receive the warning of our Lord.

God again reminds them of His work for them as a nation, from the time of their deliverance out of Egypt, and from all the power of the enemy up to the present. He reiterates the fact that in their desire for a king they, and not He, have been the rejectors. He, blessed be His name, never turns from His people whom He has redeemed. His love to them is measured by that redemption, and all their future experience would be but repetitions, according to need, of that deliverance but, alas, how prone are His people to forget the past, and measure the present by their unbelief, rather than by His power as manifested for them again and again.

It is not, however, with any view of securing a change of mind on the part of the people. They were determined in their course. That wretched watchword "like all the nations" had gnawed into their spiritual vitals and produced its necessary results. A king they must and will have, and it must be the one who answers to such a state of heart as that. What other kind of one could it be?

God deigns still to serve His people, as we have been seeing, and to interpret their own wretched minds for them, giving expression to their desires, far better than they could themselves. For this purpose He uses the lot, leaving nothing to mere chance or to the caprice of any part of the people, still less to that modern fallacy, the will of the majority. "The lot is cast into the lap, but the whole disposing is of the Lord." It also causes contentions to cease. We cannot for a moment think that, though thus guiding in the choice, God was pleased with it, or that the man selected thus would represent His desires for the people. We have already dwelt upon this.

And now the tribes are brought up one by one, and "little Benjamin" is taken, ominously significant as one which up to this time had been distinguished chiefly by its fearful rebellion. The one who rules others must rule himself first of all, and he who claims obedience from a nation must be preeminently the obedient one. How perfectly has our blessed Lord manifested His capacity for rule in this way, resigning, as we might say, the place of authority, "taking the form of a servant," learning obedience in all His life of lowliness. Truly He has qualified Himself to be the true King of Israel as well as the Ruler and Lord of all His people.

There is no account of Benjamin's repentance, and therefore we may well suppose that the tribe was still marked by that spirit of rebellion which had wrought such havoc in the days of the judges. And yet that hardihood of spirit, that rash courage which marked them at that time—one of the least of the tribes facing the entire nation, and "giving a good account of itself" in the conflicts that ensued—was doubtless rehearsed and handed down, and became matter for boasting, rather than for humiliation and true self-abhorrence before God. Thus it will ever be with the flesh. It will boast in that which is its shame, and plume itself upon a strength which must be broken to pieces before God can come in. It thus represents, as a tribe, the nation; and while we cannot say that all this was intensified in that branch of the tribe from which Saul came, neither is there any indication of its absence.

The various families are sifted out and finally the choice falls upon Saul himself. We have already looked at his genealogy. Another name is here mentioned, the "family of Matri," which is said to mean "Jehovah is watching," which ought, at least, to have been a reminder that the holy eye of God had seen all their past, and knew well too their present. How the mention of this should have caused both the people and Saul to halt! God's holy eye was upon them. He had searched out their secret thoughts. He knew their motives, their state of soul, their self-confidence, their pride. Could they, with that holy eye of love resting upon them, proceed in this wretched course of disobedience, that which was practically apostasy from Himself? Alas, while Jehovah's eye is open upon them, theirs is closed as to Him. They have eyes only for the king whom they desire, and he is soon presented to their gaze.

The lot declares that Saul, the son of Kish, is the appointed man. But he is nowhere to be found. Flesh-like, he hides himself when he ought to be present, and obtrudes himself when he should be out of sight. Self-depreciation is a very different thing from true lowliness of spirit. As the poet says; Satan's "darling sin is the pride which apes humility." He had already spoken to Samuel of his tribe being the smallest in Israel and his family the least in that tribe. All this had been overruled by the prophet who had anointed him. He had already received the assurance that he was the appointed king. God Himself had spoken to him through the signs that we have been looking at, and in the spirit of prophecy which had indeed also fallen upon himself. Why, then, this feigned modesty, this shrinking from the gaze of his subjects? Does it not indicate one who is not truly in the presence of God? For when in His presence, man is rightly accounted of. The fear of man indicates the lack of the fear of God, and "bringeth a snare." In God's presence, the lowliest can face the mightiest unflinchingly. Hear the faithful witnesses refusing to obey the command of king Nebuchadnezzar. There is no hiding there: "We are not careful to answer thee in this matter. If it be so, our God whom we serve is able to deliver us from the burning fiery furnace; but if not, be it known unto thee, O king, that we will not serve thy gods nor worship the golden image which thou hast set up" (Daniel 3:16-18). Faith in God produces true liberty in man.

But even if this shrinking from the people did not indicate the extreme of fear, it yet showed a self-occupation which is utterly incompatible with the true spirit of rule. Saul indeed does not appear to advantage here, and we get a glimpse of his character as he hides among the baggage, which bodes ill for himself and the people.

Indeed it is the Lord Himself who must go further in this patient care for a perverse people and tell them what has become of their king. The baggage seems a strange place in which to look for royalty; not much dignity about that, and one can almost imagine the ludicrousness of the scene. No wonder that carnal men ask, a little later on, How shall this man save us? He was indeed a part of the baggage and an illustration of the old Latin word for that, "an impediment," no help, but a hindrance to those whom he should lead on to victory.

But he at least appears better than his people. Judged according to the appearance, he is "every inch a king," head and shoulders above all the rest, one to whom they could look up and in whom they could boast; and if fleshly strength were to count, one who was more than a match for any who would dare dispute his right and title to the place. Do we not all know something of this stateliness of the flesh when it stands in full length before us? Hear another son of

Benjamin describing how he stood head and shoulders above his countrymen: "If any other man thinketh he hath whereof he might trust in the flesh, I more: circumcised the eighth day, of the stock of Israel, of the tribe of Benjamin, a Hebrew of the Hebrews; as touching the law, a Pharisee; concerning zeal, persecuting the Church; touching the righteousness which is in the law, blameless" (Philippians 3:4-6). I "profited in the Jews' religion above many my equals in mine own nation, being more exceedingly zealous of the traditions of my fathers" (Galatians 1:14).

Here is another Saul, a king among men, too; but, ah how all this shrivels up under the eye of divine holiness and love; in the very noontide of his carnal greatness, he beholds One who had been crucified but now was glorified, and as he catches sight of that glorious Object on high, from the dust he can declare for the remainder of his life: "What things were gain to me, those I counted loss for Christ." Would that we ever remembered this when tempted to glory in our flesh, or measure ourselves by ourselves and compare ourselves among ourselves!

Paul was ashamed even to speak of the work of Christ in and through him, save as it was needed to deliver the poor Corinthians who were, like the Israel we are examining, tempted to judge according to the flesh. The only man in whom he could glory was the man in Christ, and well he knew that that man was "not I, but Christ." "I am crucified with Christ; nevertheless I live, yet not I, but Christ liveth in me" (Galatians 2:20).

However, there is none of this knowledge of the flesh, even in an Old Testament measure, among the people. They compare their king with themselves. He is better than they are, head and shoulders above them, and exultantly they shout aloud: "Long live the king!" They have found their man. How that cry has re-echoed down the centuries ever since! King after king has been brought into view over great or small nations, and when he is seen, his prowess, his knowledge, his ability, in some sense has been recognized as above the average; at least his position has put him upon a pedestal, and

"Long live the king!" has been the people's acclaim!

But faith can detect the wail in this exultation, and the unconscious yearning for One who is indeed the true King; One who is not to be compared with the sons of men, surely not head and shoulders above them; One who took His place as servant to the lowest, humbled even unto death, the death of the cross, and who now in His exaltation is far above all principality and power and might and dominion and every name that is named. Who could compare himself with the King, even to acknowledge His superiority? No, "my beloved is one," "the chiefest among ten thousand" "yea, He is altogether lovely."

"The shout of a king is in her"; but in this shout there is the echo of that other shout when the Ark was brought out to the camp of Israel and they supposed that God was going to link His holy name with their unrighteousness and give them victory over the Philistines. As we saw, He would rather let His glory be carried captive into the enemy's land than dishonor His name among His people. This shout is like that. We yet wait for the true shout of the King: but it will come, thank God, for Israel and for this poor, groaning earth; the time when all creation shall burst forth in the shout. "With trumpets and sound of a cornet make a joyful noise before the Lord, the King. Let the sea roar and the fulness thereof; the world and they that dwell therein. Let the floods clap their hands; let the hills be joyful together before the Lord, for He cometh to judge the earth. With righteousness shall He judge the world."

The scene, however, is not allowed to close with mere enthusiasm. This is not checked; but "the manner of the kingdom" is described, and God's will is impressed upon them, if they will but hear it, together no doubt with His warning which we have been considering. All is written in a book, to leave them without excuse; to be there, too, no doubt, for reference, should penitence or faith ever turn to it —a proof of God's faithful care, though His heart was grieved and wounded at the treatment He had received from those He had fed from His hand for so long. The book is laid up before the Lord.

Surely it is there yet. He has not forgotten. He never can forget. In His own patience He still waits, and the time is coming when all will be gone over with them and they shall acknowledge, with shame, their own folly as well as His love and faithfulness.

We, too, have the book of the Lord in which His faithful testimony as to the unprofitableness of the flesh is fully recorded. This He never forgets, and oh, may we remember always that God has put a mark upon it even as He did upon Cain, and may we shrink from every form of that exaltation of the natural man, "hating even the garment spotted by the flesh."

Saul again retires for the time, into private life. The second stage has been reached, the first being his private anointing. Still, however, opportunity must be afforded for him to make good practically that which has been publicly declared. A band of young men are touched by the hand of God and follow Saul. Many yet, however, are skeptical and ask how such an one could save them out of the hand of their enemies. The king is still despised by many of his people. There is none of the honor paid to him, no presents brought to him which would show he is enthroned in their hearts. He, however, is impressed, for a time at least, by the solemnity of all that he had been passing through, and makes no attempt to vaunt himself or claim a place which was not willingly accorded to him. He holds his peace and waits a suited time. Had he continued to do this, a different history would follow.

The occasion is not long wanting to show what manner of man the new king is. With the nation prone to wander from God, as the whole book of Judges shows, attacks were constantly invited by the enemy from various quarters. Morally, their condition was unchanged from the times of the Judges; and, as is abundantly shown in that book, so far from there being true progress, the periods of captivity increase as the years roll on. Nature never improves with time. It can only deteriorate. However, there was some gracious recovery on God's part, of the people, which preserved them from complete disintegration. But the constant danger when they were left to themselves was from the hands of enemies, who were all too ready to take advantage of every weakness. The outbreak narrated now was significantly on the east side of Jordan, in Gilead, and by the Ammonites, kinsmen according to the flesh, of Israel.

Remembering that the whole settlement of the two tribes and a half on the east side of Jordan was practically dictated by self-interest, that they seemed never fully to be identified with the mass of the nation on the west side of the river, it can easily be gathered that there was less devotedness to God there than even in the proper inheritance of the people. Looking at it spiritually, it is, of course, very significant. Settling down in the world, allowing selfish interests to dictate our path and testimony, is to open the gates for the enemy's assail. Alas, how frequently this is done, and what subtle tendencies there are in our hearts to repeat it!

These two tribes and a half are finally carried captive before even the remnant of the kingdom of Israel. They would answer, in that way, to the hindmost of the people in the march through the wilderness, who were specially exposed to the assaults of Amalek.

It is also worthy of note that the men of Jabesh Gilead, who were the special object of the assault in this case, had refused to unite with the rest of the nation in revenging the awful iniquity of Gibeah in which the tribe of Benjamin was involved. There is a significant connection in this, at which we will look later on.

As to Ammon, the assailing power, as has been said, he was a descendant of Lot and related, according to nature, with the people whom now he would overthrow; and so far from this forming any tie of affection, it was really the occasion of special hatred, as the history will show. Moab and Ammon are the inveterate enemies of Israel, constantly threatening and frequently bringing them into subjection. Spiritually speaking, we have learned to dread that which can claim a sort of kinship to the things of God without being truly His. Thus, Judaism was the bitterest enemy of Christianity, and at the present time everything that apes the true faith of God is all the more dangerous, because of a certain external similarity. Satan's weapon, liar that he is, is dissimulation. He makes a counterfeit, with which he assails the truth, as Jannes and Jambres, by imitating it.

As has been seen in the book of Judges, Moab and Ammon represent the two sides of the flesh: Moab, an empty profession, accompanied by carnal indulgence, as seen in Eglon their king (see Judges 3:17-25); and Ammon, living further north, with, apparently more vigor, answering rather to intellectual perversion and the intrusion of doctrinal evil into the things of God.

What would complete this array of fleshly religionists is the Philistines, who represent the religion of the flesh, as Moab does its profession, and Ammon, its doctrines.

The king of Ammon is Nahash, which primarily means "serpent," and, in that connection, suggests the thought of sorcery and divination and other Satanic practices. Thus, the association of evil doctrine with its author is clearly seen. The serpent was more subtle than any of the beasts of the field. It is the cunning of Satan which has mingled together some outward forms of truth with the deadly poison of error. We need only to look about us at the present time to see the Ammonites, under the leadership of their cunning king. False doctrines of every kind flourish under the very shadow of Christianity, and bearing its name. In fact, these, so far from decreasing as the knowledge of Scripture increases, seem to multiply. Satan has many forms of untruth, all alike proceeding from the common source. These, then, would represent the enemy now attacking a portion of the nation of Israel; that portion, as we have seen, which was most exposed to such an assault, but least able to cope with it.

We must notice also another thing in striking similarity with the revival of a power which also, to some extent, resembles that of Ammon. It will be remembered that in the time of Joshua, Jabin, king of Hazor, was completely overthrown and his capital laid in ruins. Notwithstanding this, again we find the same enemy, with the same name, revived in the times of the Judges, threatening the people with destruction, as though he had never been overthrown. This is characteristic of evil, of that which assails doctrinal truth. Jabin stands for the spirit of infidelity, and Ammon, as we have just been seeing, is the same spirit of untruth, only applied more intimately to the doctrines of God's word.

As Jabin had once been overthrown, so Ammon had been completely conquered by Jephthah during the Judges; and yet we find him here re-asserting his power with all the vigor of the early day. All this scarcely needs any comment in the way of spiritual application. We know too well how ancient heresies revive, and how it is not sufficient to have overcome them once. They must be ever kept beneath the feet of God's people, or they will quickly reassert themselves and bring havoc and destruction. At the present day, very many of the blasphemous doctrines which are being held and taught under the name of Christian truth, are the revival of old heresies which were apparently exploded centuries ago. This shows a perennial activity in things of evil, which must be met by a perennial vigor of faith far greater than the evil which it opposes.

Nahash is sufficiently insolent in his demands upon the men of Jabesh Gilead to awaken in them any slumbering manhood but this seems impossible. He is not satisfied with their subjugation. He will rob them of their eyesight, taking away their right eye, and lay this as a reproach upon the whole nation of Israel. Thus we see the pride which is not satisfied with the local triumph, but would array itself against the entire mass of God's people. And it is just in these ways that Satan overreaches himself. He seems never to have learned, in all the centuries of his experience and with all the power of his cunning, to control that malice which, after all, is the strongest feature of his character.

It has been suggestively remarked that the right eye would speak of faith, as the left would of reason. So far from being fanciful, this seems perfectly simple. The right is the place of priority and importance, and surely faith is above reason; and yet reason has its place even in the things of God. We are not deprived of that, but where it is under the control of faith, reason can put forth all its powers without danger of leading us astray.

The challenge of Nahash, then, would be that faith is to be sacrificed. That which they know to be the truth of God is to be given up, and this is to be laid as a reproach upon all the people of God. And surely is not this the case? Wherever faith is compelled to close its eyes, it is a shame upon the saints of God throughout the world. Alas, how much there is to bring the blush to our cheek as we see how many reproaches have been laid upon us!

The men of Jabesh apparently have little hope, but are not ready to submit to this loss and indignity without at least an appeal to one who had been pointed out by God as a leader and deliverer for them. Thus they ask for a seven days' respite, and send for succor to Saul.

After his public recognition, Saul had returned to the privacy of his daily work and is here found by the messengers from Jabesh Gilead. The humiliating story of the threat of Nahash produces in the people at least sorrow, if not indignation, but there are no stirrings of faith, only a helpless lamenting that such things should be possible. It is different, however, when Saul returns from his labor in the field. Inquiring what the cause of their grief is, he is told the shameful story; there is no weeping on his part, but rather the righteous indignation of God by His Spirit against the insolence of the enemy.

As we said, Saul shows well here. He passes from service into conflict, and the one is a fitting preparation for the other. However, certain things are wanting, which are suggestive. In the first place, let it be noticed that the Spirit of God may come upon one in whom He has not effectually wrought for salvation. The Old Testament gives instances of this, notably in the case of Balaam, who declares the whole mind of God as to Israel, while himself willing to pronounce a curse upon them, and, in fact, afterwards plotting for their overthrow. Thus, it must not be understood that the Spirit that moved Saul was anything more than the external power which the Spirit of God put upon him in connection with his official place. The threat, also, against the people, with the bloody message evidenced through the oxen hewn in pieces, does not savor of that dignity of faith which alone endures. Threats may energize into temporary faithfulness and spasmodic courage, but it is only the inward abiding which can produce lasting results for God. Then, too, we see that Saul is still leaning upon another arm than that of God, even though it be the arm of the faithful servant of the Lord, Samuel. The threat is, that "Whosoever cometh not forth after Saul and after Samuel, so shall it be done unto his oxen." Samuel never claimed a place of equality with the new king. He was perfectly willing to be his servant and that of Jehovah, and it does not look as though Saul fully realized how his relations were to be directly with the Lord, without any human intervention whatever.

However, there is, at any rate, thorough earnestness for the time being, and a real purpose to deliver Israel; and this God recognizes—as He ever does in whatever measure He can, a turning to Himself. Multitudes respond to the threatening call and are gathered after Saul. A reassuring message is sent to the men of Jabesh Gilead, and all is ready for the deliverance. Saul shows skill and wisdom in disposing his army in three companies. There is an absence of precipitateness which argues well. The early rising, too, before daylight, shows an intentness of purpose and prudence in taking the first step, which always is a presage of victory.

This reminds us of some of the old conflicts of days gone by, under Abraham and Joshua. In fact, it was under the same leadership, though perhaps with people not so willing and ready as in those days. The result is not for a moment in any uncertainty. Ammon is thoroughly discomfited, his vast hosts beaten down and multitudes destroyed, while the remainder are scattered to the winds, no two remaining together. Thus, the proud flesh, with its knowledge and insolence, is overthrown. Heresy, false doctrine, cannot stand before an attack like this. It is quite significant that King Saul should be more successful in this conflict with the Ammonites than in any of his subsequent wars. There was that in him which peculiarly fitted him, typically speaking, for such warfare.

After all, a successful conflict with doctrinal evil is not the highest form of victory. The history of the Church has shown men who were vigorous contestants for doctrinal truth and scriptural exactness, who had, alas, but little heart for the Lord Jesus, and little in their lives that would commend Him. A certain form of the flesh may, for the time being, take special pleasure in overthrowing error. Jephthah, who had previously conquered the Ammonites, showed that a victory over false doctrine can go with bitter hatred of one's brethren; and of this, too, we have illustrations in the history of the Church. Doctrinal contentions that sprang up in connection with the great work of the Reformation are the common shame of Protestantism.

However, the victory is won, and God can be thanked for it. The people, in that revulsion of feeling which is common to human nature, wish to know who it was that had opposed Saul being appointed king. They are ready to put them to death at once, when perhaps multitudes of themselves had looked with much suspicion upon him.

Saul, however, checks all this, and still shows well in his ascribing the glory of the victory to Jehovah; at the same time he would show perfect clemency to his enemies. There is wisdom as well as mercy in this.

Samuel, however, goes further. He calls the people back: "Come and let us go to Gilgal and renew the kingdom there." Strikingly fitting place indeed was it for all to return to. The normal camping ground after every victory, as we remember in Joshua's day, it is the true place to which we should ever come. Gilgal teaches the great lesson of the sentence of death upon ourselves, having no confidence in the flesh. It was the true circumcision, where the reproach of Egypt was rolled off, the first camping ground in the land after the people had crossed Jordan. It thus emphasizes, as we were saying, the great truth of the Cross applied practically to our lives and persons. It was the one lesson which the nation as a whole needed to learn in fuller measure than they had yet done, and which, for Saul, as their leader and representative, was absolutely indispensable.

So, it is a call of mercy which is hearkened to externally, and all congregate at Gilgal. Here Saul is again made king in connection with sacrifices of peace-offerings. It is rather significant that these are the only offerings mentioned. Nothing is said whatever of the burnt or sin-offering. The peace-offering speaks of fellowship with God and with one another; the burnt-offering, of the infinite acceptability of Christ, in His death, to God; while the sin-offering tells how He has borne our sins and put them away. Communion cannot be the first thought. It is appropriate, at Gilgal particularly, where death to the flesh comes in, that there should be prominent mention of that death of the cross which has put away sin and which is infinitely precious in God's sight. However, peace-offerings show at least a unity of fellowship, which, as far as it goes, is good. We read that Saul and all Israel rejoiced greatly. Poor man, would that that joy had had a deeper root! It would have borne more abundant and abiding fruit. Nothing is said of Samuel's joy. Doubtless it was there in some measure, though perhaps chastened as he remembered the cause of their being there. He could not forget, spite of all this brave show and recent victory, that the people had rejected the Lord, and that the man before them was not the man of God's choice, but of their own.

They had come to Gilgal at the invitation of Samuel to renew the kingdom; and this he proceeds to do in the divine, rather than in the human way. Man's thought of reorganization, or renewal, is to strengthen everything on the basis upon which it rests. The people evidently had this in mind in connection with the celebration of their victory over the Ammonites, and the joy which accompanied it. Samuel, however, appropriately with the place, seeks to lead the people into deeper self-judgment, goes back indeed to the roots which had made possible their present condition, and shows how their desire for a king was connected with their sin and departure from God.

First of all, he speaks of himself. He is about to lay aside that government which, as judge, he had exercised for God. There was no longer need for a judge if they had a king. How significant it was that there was still the same need for him as ever, showing the utter incompetence of the king, who occupied a place officially which he could not actually fill! Samuel spreads his whole life before them, going back to his childhood days, when he had taken his place publicly before the nation as one who was to be a servant for God. From that day to the present he had walked before them. His sons also were with them. Of these indeed, as we have already seen, not much could be said, and yet the very contrast of their unfaithfulness with his uprightness would only serve to bring into bolder relief the integrity which had marked his entire course. He asks them to witness against him, even as Paul did at a later day. Had covetousness, self-interest in any of its forms, characterized him? Whom had he defrauded? Whom had he oppressed? From whom had he received a bribe, that he might pervert justice? It is the last opportunity the people will have of having their wrongs righted, if indeed there were such. What a sense of integrity must have filled his heart thus to challenge their accusations!

Not even calumny can raise its voice against this faithful old man. His pure, unselfish life spoke for itself, and they can only reply, "Thou hast not defrauded us nor oppressed us, neither hast thou taken aught out of any man's hand." He calls God to witness that they have made this statement; and in thus silently passing over rule to the hands of Saul, he calls him also to witness that there has been nothing unjust in all his past life. Again the people reply, "God is witness." Will they be able to say the same of the young king, flushed with his recent victory, and the man of their choice? Will he prove as unselfish, as devoted, as single-eyed, as this aged servant of God, whose care is not so much for his own good name as for the honor of that gracious God whose servant and representative he has been? Samuel would have shrunk from the thought that he in any way had been a king. All his authority was derived from God; all his appeal was to God, and he had never sought to interpose between the people and their direct obedience to their rightful King and Ruler,

Jehovah.

This is ever the character of all true rule. Self is obliterated. If it speak of its own faithfulness, it is simply to silence false accusation, and to awaken conscience. Thus Paul, in the eleventh and thirteenth chapters of 2 Corinthians, is compelled to speak of his own course, but is well-nigh ashamed to do so. It is only to leave the Corinthians without excuse as to the character of ministry there had been amongst them.

True service, as we have said, ever has clean hands. Love, which is the spring of all service, "seeketh not her own." Fruit-bearing is for others, and not for our own enjoyment. Samuel never sought a place nor claimed dignities for himself. It was his one desire to witness for God and to be a help to His beloved people. This his whole well-spent life testified to.

It is a searching question for us: What is our motive in ministering to the saints of God? Is it simply for the honor of our Lord and for the blessing of His people, or does self enter, as an important element, into it all? The Lord keep us in that true lowliness of spirit which desires simply the blessing of others!

Having cleared his own skirts and secured from the people themselves a witness of his integrity, Samuel next speaks of the faithfulness of God, and with it of the unfaithfulness of His people. He goes back, as he had once before done, to Egypt, and rapidly reviews the salient features of their history. In their distress in Egypt they had cried to Him. Had He failed them? He sent Moses and Aaron to deliver them out of their bondage and bring them into the place which they were now occupying. Moses and Aaron were not kings. They were God's instruments accomplishing His will; but so far from displacing Him, they were the means of preserving the people in closer relationship with Himself. So, too, in the trials which had beset them since their entering into the land: all these trials were produced by their own departure from God, and He had never delivered them into the hands of enemies save when they had forsaken Him. But even when, in faithfulness, He was compelled to turn them over to such enemies as Sisera in the north, or the Philistines in the west, or the Moabites on the east, it had only been that they might learn the difference between serving God and serving evil. It would only intensify in their souls the absolute necessity of cleaving to the Lord in true-hearted obedience. As soon as they had begun to learn their lesson, how quickly did He respond to their cry! He had sent them one deliverer after another. Gideon, Jephthah, Barak, and Samuel himself, amongst others, had been used of God to rescue them from the most cruel bondage. But, as we have already seen, did these deliverers become kings? Gideon distinctly refuses the crown, and even Jephthah, though he apparently dallied with it, never usurped full kingly authority; and as to Samuel, we have already seen.

Their past lessons should have taught the people, surely, both the cause of their trouble and the way of escape. What deliverance could be more brilliant and complete than that of Gideon, or of Barak? Was anything lacking in it? Had not Samuel led them victoriously against the Philistines? Could a king do more than these had done? And yet, when a fresh evil menaces them, caused unquestionably by the same spirit of departure from God, they turn now to other relief than to the living God. The Ammonites assail, and instead of crying to God with confession of the sin which had made such an assault possible, they ask for a king, thus displacing Him who was King in Jeshurun. How faithfully the aged prophet shuts the people up to a sense of their folly! They cannot escape it. They have turned away from the One who has been their Saviour and Deliverer from Egypt to that present time. They have dishonored and rejected Him, and now they may look at their king. Surely his stature and goodly appearance would shrivel into nothingness in the presence of the mighty God whom the prophet had been holding up before them. Surely, if there was a heart to hearken, such a review as this could not fail to bring them to that true self-abasement which answers to Gilgal.

He has now unburdened himself, and therefore next speaks of the future. Even though they have thus slighted the Lord, let the time past for all this suffice, and let them with their king now go on in obedience to His will; for, after all, the king, as the people, must be subject to God. If so, they will find that His path is still open for them, and blessing will follow them; but if they turn away from Him, and refuse the voice of the Lord, and depart from Him, His hand will be against them, and they will go on to the bitter end, to learn that God is as true as His word, and that departure from Him can only bring one result.

But he will not leave them even with this last word alone. There must be visible manifestation that he is speaking for God, and that God will speak with him. It is the time of their wheat harvest, a season when all nature seems at rest; but in answer to his cry, God will send storm and thunder as tokens of His displeasure at His people's course—a witness of His resistless majesty and power. As at Sinai, the people tremble. Alas, the flesh can only tremble in the presence of God. It cannot profit by the solemn lessons of His majesty. Its one desire is to get out of that Presence, that it may do its own will. So they seem contrite enough for the time being. They acknowledge their sin in having desired a king, and ask God's mercy. Alas, all this too is superficial, as is abundantly seen in a short time.

The prophet has not meant to overwhelm them, but only to test them. And so comes the reassuring word "Fear not: ye have done all this wickedness: yet turn not aside from following the Lord, but serve the Lord with all your heart."

How patient and long-suffering is our gracious God! He will test the flesh down to the last, give opportunity after opportunity to see if there is still any true desire to cleave to Him. The prophet's one anxiety is that the people should not depart from God. There is no danger that the Lord would forsake them. For His own great name, for that grace which has set its love upon them, He will not depart from them. They are His people. The very chastenings which fall upon them are but a proof of this, and so far as He is concerned they can rest assured that His love will be with them to the end. So, too, the aged prophet will ever remain loyal to the people dearer to him than his own life. It would be a sin against God to cease to pray for them. He will continue, therefore, to be their intercessor, though they have rejected him as their leader. How beautiful and gracious is all this! Into his retirement the servant bears no grudge against an ungrateful nation. He enters simply into his closet, there to pour into the willing ear of a loving God the needs of this foolish, self-confident, fickle people.

How beautifully all this speaks of the unchanging purpose of God and the grace of our Lord Jesus Christ, we need hardly say. All on that side is secure: divine love and power pledged to bring us safely through, even in spite of the folly which would forget that grace alone can preserve. Our Intercessor abides before God, and bears His people's names and needs before His Father. So, too, will it be with all true ministry for God. One will not be soured by the indifference of those whom he is seeking to help. If he has truly been ministering for God, he will continue to pray for those who, for the time being, have no desire for his service, and are glorying in the flesh.

How the prophet rings the changes on his message! "Only fear the Lord, and serve Him in truth with all your heart; for consider how great things He hath done for you"—words surely that need not exposition, but the impress of the Holy Spirit upon our own souls! How great things has He done for us! Shall we then for a moment boast in that flesh which He condemned by the cross?

Lastly, there is a final word of warning: "But if ye shall still do wickedly, ye shall be consumed, both ye and your king." How solemnly this was fulfilled in their later history, the captivity of many a king, with the people too, makes only too manifest.

CHAPTER 8
TESTED AND FOUND WANTING

1 Samuel 12–14

We come now to that which manifests the character of the new king in a far more searching way than was possible in the matter of the children of Ammon, and this for two reasons. The enemy, the Philistines, were nearer at hand and had had a longer and more complete hold upon Israel than the enemy on the east. Saul also was to be tested as to his dependence upon God, and patient waiting brings out the inherent unbelief of the heart more quickly than activity. The nature of the Philistine oppression has already been dwelt upon, and therefore there is little need to enlarge upon it again. We need only remark how natural such a state of bondage is where such a man as Saul is reigning. He exemplifies the condition of the people at large, and this is, after all, in a spiritual sense, Philistinism itself. The flesh can be religious. We shall find this as we go on with Saul. Philistinism stands for the religiousness of the flesh, and therefore is fittingly that which oppresses those who are walking according to the flesh. On the other hand, there is an apparent resistance of this enemy, with but little power, however.

After the scene at Gilgal, which we have dwelt upon, there was an apparent season of quiet, as suggested in the first verse of the thirteenth chapter. All Israel have returned to their various homes, save 3,000 men, chosen to be the personal guard about Saul; 2,000 of these are with himself, and 1,000 with Jonathan. We have here the first mention of that beautiful character whose presence relieves the gloom of Saul's history, and the pride and self-righteousness which developed apace. Jonathan was altogether a lovely character, a man of genuine faith and devotedness to God; as unlike his father as it is possible to conceive. It will be a pleasure to trace his course, which is brought into clearer relief by contrast with his father's.

Jonathan is really the forerunner of David, and in a marked way he is merged into the man after God's own heart. We will doubtless have occasion to speak of him in other respects at the proper time, but unquestionably the main lessons of his life are most profitable and attractive. From the very beginning, he takes the initiative against the proud enemy, and smites their garrison in Geba the fortified hill.

Of course this was most audacious on the part of a subject people, as evidently the Israelites had become, even so soon after the deliverance effected by Samuel. The Philistines hear of it, and naturally begin at once to move against the people who were even in such little measure as this bestirring themselves. Faith does not fear to strike, no matter how absolute the oppression. Formalism may have laid its deadly hand upon the saints of God so completely that none dare lift his voice in protest; but faith will smite wherever there is an opportunity. It does not coldly calculate the effect, nor count up the numbers the enemy will be able to bring into the field to crush it. It counts rather upon God alone. Here is that which is not according to Him,—it must be denounced—it must be smitten. Such faith was that exhibited on many a page of Church history, where some genuine soul has seen and smitten abuses which had become so entrenched that it seemed an impossibility that God's people could ever be delivered from them, and what results have followed!

As we said, it is Jonathan who does this, and not Saul; but he will be at least a second in such work. His own pride, perhaps also a real interest on his part, would lead him not to be behindhand. He blows the trumpet, therefore, to assemble all Israel, saying: "Let the Hebrews hear." He does not use the familiar name "Israel," which had so many blessed suggestions in it; but rather the natural name of the people, going back to their descent from Abraham, the Hebrew. Of course there is a spiritual use of the word "Hebrew" which suggests pilgrim character, but this evidently is not in Saul's mind. He simply arrayed the nation of Hebrews against the Philistines. But there does not seem the same energy and decision that marked him in the case of Ammon. There, he would take no refusal of the people, but urged them with threats to go out with him and Samuel against the enemy. He is evidently on even lower ground here than there. Israel also hears the report of this preliminary victory of Jonathan, only ascribing it to Saul, as the prowess of many a subordinate has been ascribed to his commanding general.

The state of the people, however, is sadly brought out by the manner of their reception of the news, So far from it thrilling them with vigor and arming them as one man now to make an end of this proud enemy, they are filled with terror. They realize that they are now held in abomination by the Philistines, and are more occupied with that than the possibility of their deliverance from them. How like unbelief in all time is this! It fears the consequences of any measure of faithfulness. "Knowest Thou that the Pharisees were offended, after they heard this saying?" said the disciples to our Lord when He had been boldly denouncing the formalism of the leaders of the people. They were afraid of the consequences of such faithfulness; and while perhaps acknowledging the truth of what our Lord had said, shrank from stirring up opposition. Alas, we know much of this timidity in view of opposition. What will men say? What will our friends say? Oh, how often has this deterred many an one whose conscience has been awakened as to his path, from going on in simple obedience to God, regardless of what men say! Truly, "the fear of man bringeth a snare;" and to be occupied with the effect of our action upon the enemies of God, rather than with Himself, is indeed to invite defeat.

Truly the Philistines had gathered together in enormous numbers to fight with Israel; chariots and horsemen and people as the sand on the seashore, a most formidable host: and if they have only conferred with flesh and blood, no wonder the children of Israel are terror-stricken. This is too sadly the case: and the people, instead of boldly confronting this host, remembering that it was against the Lord that they had come forth and not against His feeble people, they flee to the caves, and hide in the thickets and rocks, in high places and pits. Some of them also flee further yet, over to the east side of Jordan and the land of Gad and Gilead, and there is apparently utter nervelessness in the whole nation.

Poor material indeed is this, and yet doubtless many amongst this terror stricken people were groaning with the sense of the dishonor done to God by their subjection to this enemy.

Saul, at least, does not follow the people in their hiding. In fact, he abides at Gilgal, the place which Samuel had appointed for the meeting with himself, which was soon to take place. During all the time that had intervened between his anointing and the present, there had not been the real opportunity to manifest his true obedience to the prophet's directions (1 Samuel 10:8).

Saul is at Gilgal, where, had he truly entered into the spirit of the place, he would have found an impregnable position, and from which he could have gone forth victoriously to triumph over all the host of the enemy. A few follow him also, so tremblingly that evidently their eye is upon their human leader, and they have forgotten the living God. This wretched remnant of an army is really a mockery of any true resistance, and would have been found so, had it been tested. Even this little handful, Saul is not able to hold together. He must, according to the prophet's directions, remain seven days, or until Samuel appears to offer the appointed sacrifices. Surely without these, it would be madness to attempt to meet the enemy. It must be ever on the basis of a sacrifice that we dwell with God, and from the strength of His presence go out to meet the enemy. Saul recognizes this in his way, and evidently waits with impatience the coming of the prophet. Meanwhile, the people are melting away and he will be left alone, and this the flesh cannot endure. It has not God before it, and therefore must look upon apparent resources. With his army gone, what could the king do? Surely, God would not have this: therefore he must take some steps to inspire confidence in the people, and be prepared to go forth to fight.

Alas, we know something, doubtless, in our own experience, of this restlessness of the flesh, which recognizes that something must be done, but never does the only thing that is suitable,—wait upon God for His time.

So, Saul offers the sacrifices, intruding himself in this way into the priest's office and practically ignoring all need of that which was at the basis of sacrifice, a mediator. The flesh, with all its religiousness and punctiliousness, never grasps the fact that it has no standing before God. It would intrude into the holiest things, and, as we have already said, this is the very essence of Philistinism, which would thrust nature into the presence of God, and, according to its own thoughts, build up a system of approach to Him which would at the same time quiet natural conscience and foster the pride of the unregenerate heart.

This was an awful fall for the king. It was the very thing against which the prophet had guarded him in the beginning; the very thing, too, which was the peril of the people,—acting without God. Their choice of a king had really been this, and therefore all is in fitting keeping with that act of independence. Saul had had ample warning, abundant opportunity to manifest his faith and obedience if he had any. The very place where he was had but lately witnessed the solemn testimony of Samuel, and heard the voice of Jehovah in thunder at the time of harvest. Had the fear of God really filled his soul, it would have eclipsed all other fear, and the king would have waited patiently, though he waited alone, for the word from the Lord. But he is tested and fails. So soon as the failure occurs, in divine mercy on the one hand, and justice on the other, Samuel appears on the scene.

What unavailing regrets doubtless filled Saul's bosom as he saw the prophet! Oh, had he only waited but a few moments longer! But this is not the point. God would test him to see whether he would wait. He had not almost held out, but he had simply manifested the state of his soul. There is no such thing as almost obeying the Lord. The heart that is truly His, will obey; and testing, no matter how far carried, will never bring out disobedience from a heart that is truly subject to God. How perfectly this was brought out in the life of our blessed Lord, who was constantly subjected to pressure in one form or another to depart from the path of simple obedience to God. There was no danger of waiting too long in His case. All the testing would only bring out the reality of that obedience which controlled His whole spirit, and He is the only true King of men, the only Man after God's heart to lead His people; and it is only as His Spirit fills our souls, that we will walk in His steps, having the mind in us which was in Christ.

Saul runs out officiously to greet the prophet, as he does in a more marked way after a still deeper failure a little later on; but there is no responsive greeting from the dear faithful servant of God whose soul burned with indignation at the king's palpable unbelief and disobedience. Sternly he asks, "What hast thou done?" He need not go further with his question, nor can Saul pretend to be ignorant of what is meant. What he had done was in known violation of the prophet's word. Therefore he had practically forfeited all claim upon the prophet's service or the approval of God. He, however, puts up a feeble defense; and notice the character of that defense. "I saw that the people were scattered from me." In other words, his eye was on the people, who were as full of unbelief as himself, instead of upon God. Then, Samuel had not come during the appointed days. This, as we have already seen, was simply to test the genuineness of his faith.

And lastly, the Philistines were gathering together in great numbers. Not a word, we notice, of the Lord. Now, however, he says the enemy will come down to attack him (a most unlikely thing for an enemy to do in such a place as Gilgal) and he must make supplication unto the Lord. At last the Lord is brought in, but we notice that it is only in this feeble way. Really what filled the foreground of the king's vision was the melting of the people, the menace of the enemy's attack, and the absence of the human prop in Samuel. So he says: "I forced myself therefore, and offered a burnt-offering." How many have fallen in the same way! His words are a confession that he knew he had disobeyed God in offering the sacrifices. It was contrary, he would have Samuel believe, to his own inclinations. He had to do it in spite of his convictions and desires. All the more, then, did it fully manifest the unbelief which will not cling to God, at all costs, in obedience. How much is excused in the same way! Human expedients are condoned, fleshly activity is encouraged, fellowship with the world is allowed, all under the plea of expediency. The reluctant conscience has to be forced, for it knows that these things are contrary to God; but force itself it will, if not subject to God in living faith.

In a minor way, how saints of God may dishonor Him in the assembly of His people by allowing the flesh to dictate what shall be done. It knows that what is being done is not according to God, and yet, for fear of man, forces itself to fall in with what others are doing. Thus, the Spirit is quenched and grieved. This will ever be the case where the flesh is allowed to dictate.

Samuel's reply is startlingly frank. Saul has done foolishly. He does not attempt to take up his reasons in detail. The people may have been scattered. He does not refer to that. The enemy may be threatening. He does not even explain his own tarrying, though its purpose was manifest. One thing he has to say to the king: "Thou hast not kept the commandment of the Lord thy God which He commanded thee." How all his paltry excuses are scattered to the winds by that solemn arraignment! What excuse can there be for disobedience? Then, too, as to the consequences of this they were not temporary, nor would they be immediately manifested, but this act had shown him to be utterly incapable of rule, to be certainly not the man after God's heart. If indeed he had stood this test, his kingdom would have been established, for it would have been seen that he was a man of genuine faith. One thing he lacked, and that one thing was absolutely needful. It was really everything. It was faith in God. Everything else may be present, but where this is wanting, one cannot be used of Him.

His kingdom, therefore, shall not continue. God must have a man after His own heart; one who knows Him and His goodness and love, and who, spite of many shortcomings, still has a true spirit of obedience to God, which springs from confidence in Him. A little later on will see poor Saul with wonderful zeal and rigidness of external obedience; but we will notice always that wherever the will of God came in conflict with the wishes of man or the desires of his own heart, Saul was wanting. How unspeakably sad and solemn is this, yea, how searching to our hearts! God grant that it may search out every vestige of self-confidence in us, every particle of unbelief which would turn us from obeying God rather than man!

Having delivered his faithful witness to the king, nothing further holds Samuel at Gilgal. The place had lost, for the time being at least, its spiritual significance—the state of the king little answering to it. We hear of the prophet no more, for Samuel though, as we know, his heart was sorely grieved at the development of evil—cannot go on with it. He apparently withdraws to the same place, Gibeah of Benjamin, whither Saul comes; but as no mention is made of any intercourse between them there, it is probable that the prophet did not tarry long.

The people have dwindled down to a paltry 600; enough surely, if they were with God, to do all the works which David with a like number did later on; but the one thing needful is lacking. They abide in Gibeah of Benjamin, near Saul's native place, and with painful suggestions of the past associated with it. The Philistines encamp in all their power at Michmash—as Young gives it, "the place of Chemosh," or, translating the latter name, "a fire," answering to the desolation which marked their occupation of the land—a burnt-over territory with no verdure or fruit.

From this center they devastate the entire land. One company goes to Ophrah, the city of Gideon, to the land of Shual, "the jackal;" very significant in this connection, for surely wild beasts were devouring the heritage of Israel.

Another goes to Beth-horon, "the house of destruction;" and still another passes on across the land until they can look down into the valley of Zeboim, where all fertility had been quenched with the fire from heaven, at the time of the destruction of Sodom. Thus, fittingly, from Michmash, "the place of fire," radiates that which consumes all the fair heritage which God had given them. How true it is that religious formalism burns up every Christian thing, every sign of real life to God!

How are the people to meet this devastating horde? Their pitiable condition is seen in the fact that there was no smith found throughout all the land. The Philistines had taken them away to prevent them from manufacturing weapons of war for the Israelites. Even for the peaceful pursuits of agriculture they were dependent upon their masters, and were obliged to go down to them to have their plowshares sharpened, or the ax, or even the mattock. Nothing remained for them but a file for the mattocks and plows, which could put but a poor and temporary edge upon their implements. We are reminded of the lament of Deborah over the condition of the people in her day: "Was there a shield or spear seen among 40,000 in Israel?"

Can it be possible that these are the people who have, but a short time ago, gone so valiantly against their enemies? Their condition is pitiable. They have been reduced to a worse condition than servitude, being dependent upon their masters even for the means of tilling the soil. But more pitiable is the spiritual condition of the people of God when under similar circumstances. Wherever the power of formalism prevails, as seen in its completeness in Rome, not only are all spiritual weapons taken out of the hands of God's people, but even the needful spiritual implements for cultivating the peaceful means of satisfying our soul's hunger are removed. Our inheritance is a spiritual one. We are "blessed with all spiritual blessings in heavenly places in Christ," and this answers, as we know, to Israel's position in Canaan; but the soil, though fruitful and drinking of the water of the rain of heaven, needed to be cultivated if it were to yield its increase. So, too, in spiritual things. There is no lack in what is ours in Christ. As far as the eye of faith can reach—north, south, east and west—all is ours, and every part that the foot of faith treads upon practically belongs to the saints; but if the soil is not cultivated, of what use is it? We might say that our inheritance is contained in the precious word of God, and that our cultivation of this, the diligent digging beneath the surface for its precious things, the turning it over with the plow of conscience, applying it thus to ourselves, answers to the various agricultural pursuits indicated here. The domination of religious formalism would rob us of the means of doing this. Need we ask, with how many of us does our portion lie fallow because we are apparently without implements for its cultivation? The Bible, in other words, is a closed book; or, if read, seems to be but barren because there is no searching into its wondrous depths; or, if there is this, alas, how the dullness of our spiritual implements, our diligence, our faith, our spiritual judgment, prevents anything like a full yielding of an abundant harvest! To be sure, there is the rubbing of the file, as iron sharpeneth iron through mutual intercourse, which even formalism cannot completely destroy; but the fire is needed also, and the beating down of that which even in proper use becomes dulled, so that its keen edge may be again restored to it.

These smiths might well answer to what we have later in Israel's history—the schools of the prophets, places where the fire and the hammer of God's word and truth are applied under the direction of the Holy Spirit. They would thus correspond to all proper and scriptural means for developing activity among God's saints. Might we not say that, in their place, institutions of learning would answer to these smiths' shops, where furnishing in the knowledge of the languages in which the word of God is written, and other truths, would equip one to be a diligent seeker in the Word? Thus, schools and colleges, when in proper hands and used in faith, are most helpful in developing an ability to dig into the word of God. The same is true of all assembly fellowship. Where the Spirit of God is ungrieved, how much spiritual furnishing do we get from association together! We can see, then, what it is for all this to be in the hands of the Philistines. And has not that been the case all too often in the history of God's saints? Nay, may we not say that it is that which particularly characterizes them at the present day, religious formalism having charge of all education, both elementary and advanced, and even, in great measure, of the people of God?

A Christian parent puts his child to school and what is the character of the influence exerted over the little one there? How often is it Philistine—that which is often in open enmity against God, or so formal in character that no genuine faith is inculcated! This is seen in still greater measure when the youth passes on to college, where infidelity is taught and if his intellectual implements have a keen edge upon them, he is taught rather to turn them against the truth of God than to explore its wondrous depths.

Institutions of theological education only bring this out still more glaringly, for here the things of God are professedly the objects. Alas, higher criticism, evolution, and various forms of infidelity, are taught in the very places where one should be thoroughly furnished to cultivate the inheritance of the Lord.

We have been speaking merely of the implements used in times of peace; but when we think of the necessary weapons of warfare with which to meet the manifold enemies who are constantly threatening our heritage, here the lack is even more glaring, for not even are there dull weapons. The enemy knows too well that it will never do to leave spear and sword in the hands of those who may be nerved to use them. As we look abroad today, how many of God's people are able to meet the attacks of evil on all hands? Infidelity presses in one direction, worldliness in another, the Philistine formalism in another; and what power is there to meet it with those weapons of warfare which the apostle says are "not carnal, but mighty through God"? Surely, we can never expect Philistia to furnish weapons against itself.

In God's mercy, however, faith can triumph even here. We remember it was with an ox goad, a weapon which could be pointed up with a file, that Shamgar wrought deliverance from these very Philistines. The goad would seem to answer to those words of the wise which are as goads; a word of simple exhortation, admonition, appealing to the conscience, which true faith will ever make use of. Even Philistines cannot deprive God's people of that; and what is an ordinary and needful implement in times of peace can, in the hands of faith, be turned against the enemy with terrible effectiveness.

CHAPTER 9
SAUL AND JONATHAN CONTRASTED

1 Samuel 13:15–14:46

Wherever there is a living faith that lays hold upon God, no apparent helplessness will prevent His manifesting His power, and we have now a refreshing contrast to the timidity and helplessness of Saul and the people with him, in the energy of faith on the part of two. Jonathan, Saul's son, and his armor-bearer, act in independence of the king. Apparently seeing the uselessness of waiting for his father to take any initiative, the soul of Jonathan is stirred, and he proposes to his armor-bearer to go out alone. Saul still tarries at Gibeah, with his 600 men and with the priests, who would seem to speak of the presence of God, but whose names and connections remind us of the period of priestly ruin at the time of Eli. It is Ahiah, the son of Ahitub, Ichabod's brother, who is there. The glory had departed from Israel, and so far as these priests were concerned it had not returned. Neither Saul nor the people with him know anything of Jonathan's determination, and the priests are apparently as ignorant as the rest. How truly must faith not confer with flesh and blood, nor count upon the slightest assistance from those who have but the name without the reality of priestly communion!

Things are as discouraging as possible for Jonathan. The garrison of the Philistines is strongly entrenched upon an almost inaccessible height, separated by a deep ravine from where Jonathan was. A sharp rock on either side of this ravine would prevent his approach to the enemy, except as he had strength and courage to surmount almost impassable obstacles. The names of these two rocks are given—Bozez, which means "shining," and would dazzle the eyes and prevent any rapid climbing, while its white, bare surface would most effectually prevent any concealment needed in an ambuscade. Seneh, the sharp declivity down which he must descend before he can ascend Bozez, means "a thorn," which might easily pierce, and evidently suggests the extreme difficulty of his undertaking.

The spiritual meaning of all this seems quite clear. The enemy is strongly entrenched on its rock, surrounded by brilliant, shining heights, both intellectual and material. It would seem like madness to attempt to scale these shining heights in the hope of dislodging the proud enemy. All that can be associated with the side which is to make the attack is the barrenness, and even the apparent curse, suggested by the thorn. Is not God's hand that which has permitted all this oppression, and does it not seem like resisting Him to resist the authority of those who have gained ascendency over us under His chastening hand? But faith does not reason in this way, nor does it look at either thorns or brightness. The way of the slothful is as a hedge of thorns, but the way of faith is with God, and neither thorns nor heights are aught to Him.

Jonathan confers with his armor-bearer, who is but a young man, even nameless. He proposes to him to go over unto the camp of the Philistines. Notice how they are designated—uncircumcised people who are without the mark of covenant relationship with God, that covenant which had been made with Abraham, and the sign given to him which was ever the mark upon the Israelite. Spiritually, we know that circumcision answers to that sentence of death upon ourselves, that we should not trust in ourselves, but in the living God. It is that which was renewed at Gilgal, at which we have already looked, and speaks thus of "no confidence in the flesh." Circumcision does not trust the flesh, knows its helplessness, its hopeless enmity against God. Uncircumcision would in like manner answer to confidence in the flesh; and, after all, what are the Philistines, with all their greatness, with all their entrenchment on the shining heights of power and position? What, indeed, are they in the eyes of faith, but those who have confidence in the flesh? They trust in human power, human wisdom, human forms, everything of man, and God is left out.

What is this, after all, for faith? Does not faith know that these things cannot be trusted in, that there is no spiritual power in them whatever? So Jonathan, as he looks at them, sees only those whose confidence is false, in the arm of flesh. On the other hand, looking at God, while not absolutely sure that He will do so, he knows His ability. "There is no restraint to the Lord to save by many or by few." He sees that the battle is not his, but the Lord's. What difference does it make whether the Lord uses a host, or uses his own feeble arm? Nay, if He please, can He not act without any means? What victory already is in the air as we listen to such brave words as these, coming from a heart that is fed upon the strength of God! Is not every word true? Is there any restraint with the Lord? Can He not save by the few, as well as by the many? Has He become reconciled to His bitter enemies? Has He come under the oppression of the Philistines? To ask such questions is to answer them, and one would fain feel the quickening pulsations of a courage that partakes of Jonathan's faith.

How noble is the response of the nameless armor-bearer! "Do all that is in thy heart: turn thee; behold, I am with thee, according to thy heart." "Can two walk together except they be agreed?" And here is the faith which responds to faith, and is developed by it.

But courage does not mean rashness, though it may often seem like that. Jonathan is really working with God, as the people say later on, and therefore he must be sure that he is in God's path. He proposes, therefore, that the sign shall come from God Himself, even as Gideon in his day had his faith fortified by various signs in confirmation. Jonathan and his armor-bearer will show themselves to the Philistines. They will attract their attention. If this excites them sufficiently to come down to their position, they will stand and wait the attack. If, on the other hand, they invite them to come up to them, they will go forward in the confidence that God is leading them on to victory.

We notice, however, that no provision is made for retreating, and apparently there is nothing in his mind but a conflict and victory. It is simply a question whether he or the Philistines shall be the aggressors. Faith has its armor on the right hand and the left, has its breastplate, shield and helmet, but never any armor for the back. No provision is made for the cowardice which runs away. Jonathan will either go forward or stand his ground. He will not retreat. Neither, by God's grace, will we.

How graciously God responds to the faith that lays hold upon Him in this bold way! The two show themselves to their enemies, and are invited to come up. We can well imagine the supercilious smile of contempt with which the Philistines say, "The Hebrews come forth out of the holes where they had hid themselves." What a reproach, beloved, it is when we are afraid to say that we are the Lord's, and hide in secret places—when we are afraid to let our neighbors know that we are Christ's, and that the word of God is our sufficient guide, which we are seeking to obey! Is not such a reproach merited by the mass of the Lord's people at this time—hidden, so that even those in closest contact with them would not suspect that they are genuinely for Christ? Of course there may be, as there is, a morality and outward walk of rectitude—even to a certain extent religious observances in which Philistines themselves can join; but where is that bold confession of loyalty to Christ our Lord? Doing what we do because we belong to Christ, and not merely because it is right, or expected, or the habit of others? And when one, in the boldness and simplicity of faith, does thus show himself, speaking out frankly for his Lord's honor, how the reproach may well fall upon all the rest of the people of God if even a few are coming out of their holes and showing themselves!

But this very showing is the presage of victory. The Philistines will amuse themselves with this little morsel of opposition, and have no hesitation in inviting the bold climbers to come up to them. This they do, and a sorry day it was for the Philistines that they ever invited them up! Jonathan speaks out. The Lord has already delivered the enemy, not into his hands, mark, but into the hand of Israel; for Jonathan realizes that the victory is not for himself individually, but for all the people of God. How important it is, for all our spiritual conflicts, to realize that we are first of all fighting with God; secondly, for God; and thirdly, for all His people!

They climb up, as has been said, upon their hands and feet, suggesting both work and prayer. It is neither idleness nor vain confidence, but the toil of those who realize that in themselves is no strength. We read very little of the details of this conflict. The victory has already been won in Jonathan's heart, and further details might detract us from the real lesson involved. Faith that has conquered our own coward heart can conquer any Philistines that oppose. The slaughter does not seem to be very great, judged from human standpoint, and yet what mighty results flow from it! There is a trembling everywhere. It is as though God were laying His mighty hand upon all, and causing proud oppressors and the camp of Israel, yea, the land itself, to feel the weight of that arm which will shake not only earth, but heaven too. There is a trembling of God.

Saul and his company soon learn of the commotion among the Philistines, and of an apparent conflict and victory with which they had had nothing to do. But there does not seem to be any thought with them that God is at work—surely it must be that some of his own little company have gone to fight the enemy. "Number now, and see who has gone from us," seems to indicate that he had some idea that human power had been at work. He finds only Jonathan and his armor-bearer are absent, and this would not be sufficient to explain the commotion.

Have we not more than a hint here that the man of flesh never rises to the thoughts of faith? Could we imagine such noble words coming from Saul as we have heard from Jonathan? The flesh never rises beyond itself, its circumstances. God is left out, for in His presence it cannot exalt itself, and must be eclipsed. Even in the measure in which Saul succeeded, this was the case.

But he is now compelled to ask counsel of God, though with apparent reluctance. It is significant that the ark of God was present, as mentioned here. The camp and field was no place for it. A resting-place had been provided for it at Shiloh, where the tabernacle had been set up when Joshua brought Israel into Canaan. It had been brought out against these very Philistines in the days of Eli, with what disastrous results we know. God will never link His holy name with an unjudged state of His people. The ark went into captivity, and had never found an abiding-place since. In fact, it never did till David brought it to Zion.

Perhaps Saul was not far at this time from the hiding-place of the ark, and had had it brought as a sort of rallying-center for his dwindling band, as well as a witness that God was with him. Such expedients are not unknown to the flesh, which will make use of visible forms from which the power has departed, and seek to rally men around the names of what have become mere pretension. Rome's extreme claims are an illustration of this, though by no means the only one.

While Saul is talking with the priest, and apparently while the latter is beginning to ask counsel of God, the rout of the Philistines becomes more manifest, and the king considers this sufficient reason for discontinuing what was not his first impulse. The flesh loves not to ask counsel of God, and gladly withdraws from His presence. It looks merely at what is seen; and if victory is already assured, there is no need for dependence upon God. Alas, how common is this! We turn to God in our times of perplexity, and when all other means have failed; how readily do we dispense with His aid when there seems to be no further occasion for it! The flesh in us is as hopelessly independent of God as was this man who is a type of it. It is ever going to extremes. The man who a while ago said, "I forced myself," when intruding into what God forbade, now says, "withdraw thy hand," and turns from God, because he thinks he can get on without Him.

And yet how utterly foolish is this! Had the lesson of Ai been utterly forgotten? The feeblest enemy can conquer a people who are relying upon an arm of flesh, though flushed with past victory.

Let us remember that we need God as much in victory as in

conflict—perhaps more; for, while the issue is uncertain we naturally turn to Him, but our temptation is to forget Him when the battle is won. We must ever return to the camp at Gilgal; but as we have seen, this had no significance for poor Saul.

But God is at work, through Jonathan, and the enemy is thoroughly routed. Indeed, they turn their weapons against one another, as is so often seen in Israel's conflicts. Whenever they were with God, it was scarcely necessary for them to fight. They could "stand still," and see the enemy fighting among themselves. So it was in the days of Gideon and when Jehoshaphat faced a countless host.

Saul and his little band rush up to have a share in the battle, and join in the rout. But victory was already assured. Saul was not needed; indeed, later we find what a hindrance he was.

How good it is to see the results of a work of God like this! Not merely is the enemy overthrown, but the poor scattered sheep of Israel are called back. Many of them were captives, or willing bondsmen, to the Philistines. Many had also hidden themselves in the mountains, fearing to face the enemy. But they know a victory, and rally to the Lord's standard.

Surely it would have been faith to have needed no such recall as this, but the Lord's people are weak, "prone to wander," and easily lose sight of Him. How responsible is every one to see that his example does not encourage defection from the Lord! What a terrible thing it is to be a stumbling-block! May the Lord keep us lowly, in all self-distrust, that we do not by our example, or unbelief, scatter the feeblest of His own from Him.

But if the saints are easily scattered, they quickly rally when the Lord's hand is seen. Even in Asa's time, when division was consummated, they fell to him in great numbers out of Ephraim, when they saw that the Lord was with him.

How refreshing it is to think of these two men of faith, alone with God at the beginning, now reinforced by these scattered ones! But were they any stronger? Were not these as liable to drop off again in time of danger? Ah yes; the strength was in the Lord alone, and two with Him are infinitely stronger than the undivided host of Israel without Him. The joy is in the recovery of the wanderers; not for the help afforded by them, but rather for their own sakes, and because of the glory to the Lord's name through His people's recovery.

We must not despise numbers. Pride may lurk in the hearts of a few, as well as among the many. The strength of Jonathan and his armor-bearer was not in themselves. Their faith laid hold upon God. Apart from that they were as feeble as any of these fugitives. And these latter can in their turn be Jonathans if they but lay hold of the same One who wrought on that day.

We long to see recovery and unity among the people of God. Let us not seek to secure it in any other way than Jonathan did. It was not the ark with Saul that effected the victory, but the living faith of Jonathan which brought God in. The saints will be united, recovered from wherever they may have wandered, not by fleshly efforts to bring them together, but by turning to Him who still is the God of victory. Let us see to it that we are in all lowliness and self-distrust before Him, and the desire of our hearts for the recovery and unity of His beloved people may yet in some measure be seen.

CHAPTER 10
SAUL'S FOOLISH OATH

1 Samuel 14:23-46

Saul, having taken charge, soon turns a glorious victory into a very limited one, and, instead of the joy of conflict in God's cause, gives the people heavy hearts. He occupies them with himself rather than God, and pronounces a curse upon any who may taste food until his enemies are overthrown. He does not see God and His honor, and accordingly all takes color from this. He makes the hearts of the people sad at the very moment when they should be experiencing "the joy of the Lord."

Poor Saul! Even his religion is a gloomy, selfish thing. Like the elder brother in the parable, his service to his Father is unaccompanied even by the joy of a kid, and his friends are confessedly not his Father's. All legality is like this; self is the center and not God; and where this is the case, what can there be but depression? And its misery and discomfort is all that such a soul has to share with others. What a libel upon God's love! What a misrepresentation of Him in whose presence there is fulness of joy!

But let us again remember that Saul stands not merely for individuals, but for that principle of the flesh which is present even in the true children of God. The flesh is legal and selfish. When it intrudes into the things of God, it can only mar them. It turns the grace of God into legal claims, and even in hours of spiritual triumph would occupy the soul with itself. It has no discrimination, and would put into one common class things essentially evil and those harmless or helpful. But a little while before Saul had been glaringly disobedient to God he now goes to the other extreme, and would command "to abstain from meats which God hath created to

113

be received with thanksgiving of them which believe and know the truth."

Fasting has its place in the realm of grace as in law, but not the place given to it by legalism. Where abstinence from food is the unstudied, undemanded act of a soul absorbed with the things of God, it has a place. One might abstain from food to avoid distraction, or, in fact, because his mind is controlled by other things. But to make fasting a merit, or even to regard it as a means of grace, is to put it in somewhat the position in which Saul put it here.

See the disaster that results from this legalism. The people are passing through a wood loaded with honey. It is at their hands, just lying in their path. Jonathan, without taking his eye off the enemy, dips his staff in the honey, tastes, and is refreshed. With renewed vigor he can speed after the flying foe. When told of his father's oath, Jonathan truly characterizes the folly of it: "My father hath troubled the land." For nothing is so distracting as the legalism of the flesh.

Let us remember, too, that under plea of conscience, a morbid self-righteousness may impose its claims upon oneself and others till liberty and joy give place to groans and bondage. As we have already said, this principle is inherent in the flesh wherever found. It flourishes under the ascetic rule of the monastery, and equally so in the bosom of one who is still seeking to coerce the flesh into subjection to God, though his creed be the opposite of that of Rome. The flesh is always selfish—always; when religious—rigid and morbid. It can know nothing of the liberty of the children of God.

Jonathan takes a little honey, which speaks of the sweetness of natural things, not in themselves evil. These things must surely be approached guardedly, and taken, as it were, on the end of a rod. If we kneel down and gorge ourselves with them, as the mass of Gideon's army did, they incapacitate us for warfare. But there is much in nature that can be enjoyed by the freeborn soul without spiritual detriment. After all, "only man is vile" in the pleasing prospect about us; and scenery, the beauties of nature, needed bodily relaxation, and much else, can be a true refreshing to the Lord's wearied people. "Hast thou found honey? Eat so much as is sufficient for thee." This is the divine rule. The world, among the "all things," is ours. But we are to use it and not to abuse it, or to be brought under its power. Here grace and the Holy Spirit alone can guide and check. Needed relaxation may degenerate into the engirded loins; cheerful intercourse into unholy levity which blights true spiritual growth. We are absolutely dependent upon the Spirit of God, but He is ever sufficient.

The positive evil of Saul's fleshly restriction is soon seen. The people, faint from long abstinence rather than arduous conflict, reach historic Ajalon, scene of Joshua's long day of conflict. But, unlike him, they have been bound by mere human fetters, and have lost heart. The fear of God has left them, and they fall upon the prey and violate the first principle of sacrificial law—that all blood belonged to God. This brings in genuine defilement. The pouring out of blood (Deuteronomy 12:23–24) was ever a sort of foreshadow of that Sacrifice of "richer blood" one day to be shed. To ignore all this is defilement indeed; and this is what carnal asceticism will, by reaction, produce.

Saul here, at least outwardly, would preserve divine order, and recalls the people to the sacredness of blood. In this connection too he builds his first altar.

But the end of self-righteousness has not been reached. God has yet to put His finger upon the folly of this oath of Saul. The king proposes, and the people agree, to go down by night and spoil their enemies. But the priest suggests turning to God and seeking His mind. "Let us draw near hither to God"—a good word surely for us at all times.

And now God speaks—first, indeed, by silence, showing that it is of more importance to Him that His people should be right in their hearts than that they should pursue their enemies. This silence meant, as they knew, that some offense had been committed, and Saul rightly connects it with the oath he had imposed upon the people. But he did not yet know who the guilty person was, nor how. Like Jephthah of old, he is ready to sacrifice his child, and persuade himself he is pleasing God.

God permits all to be brought about as though Jonathan were the guilty one. The machinery, if we may so say, of the lot works out for Saul, and points at his son, And in the madness of his folly the poor king would go to the last extreme, and cut off the only man of independent faith among them.

How beautifully Jonathan shows here! He does not accuse his father, nor speak of the harshness of the oath. He frankly acknowledges his act, though he does not confess a sin. Indeed, his words imply the reverse: "I did but taste a little honey…and I must die!" How manifestly at variance with God's thoughts was such an ending to this bright life! And yet Saul is still blind. With another oath he declares Jonathan has spoken his own doom: "God do so, and more also; for thou shalt surely die, Jonathan." What can be done for a man who brings in God to carry out his own self-will, and thinks the deliverer of Israel is a malefactor? Is it not like the fatuity of the Jews at a later day, and that other Saul, of Tarsus, who invoked God's approval upon the murder of His Son, and of His people?

Saul is beyond reach, and God must interpose in another way. The people, who had so lately been demanding a king, must now withstand him. Poor Saul's authority vanishes before the hot words of a justly outraged sentiment: "Shall Jonathan die, who hath wrought this great salvation in Israel? God forbid: as the Lord liveth, there shall not one hair of his head fall to the ground, for he hath wrought with God this day." Saul is incorrigible. We do not even hear of acquiescence, nor of resistance. In sullen silence all conflict with the Philistines is abandoned, and they are permitted to return to their own territory. It has been only Jonathan's victory, and Saul has done all he could to spoil it.

We need hardly draw the evident lessons as to the flesh here. It has neither discernment of God's will, nor mercy upon those manifestly with Him. It will turn victory into defeat, put divinely-given authority to public shame by its extravagance, and turn joy into mourning and indignation. We need not go back to Israel's history for examples of this: our own hearts will furnish us with these. Oh, in how many homes has this harsh legalism broken divinely-given authority! And in how many cases has the very name of discipline become a stench because of this fleshly pretension! Need we be surprised if in such cases "the people" rise and speak?

CHAPTER 11
SAUL'S KINGDOM ESTABLISHED

1 Samuel 14:47–52

We now find Saul established in his kingdom and going on with apparent prosperity after what had previously taken place. He shows, too, considerable prowess against his various enemies. Moab as well as Ammon, the victory over whom we have already looked at, and Edom, together with the kings of Zobah and his lifelong foes the Philistines, all feel his power. It is significant that there was no complete and final overthrow of these enemies; but at any rate they were "vexed," and their assaults upon the people of God were doubtless for the time checked.

The flesh in its excellence by no means allows the unrestrained prevalence of evil. Glaring moral inconsistencies in profession, as indicated by Moab; the spirit of rationalism, as suggested in Ammon; an avowed secularity, of which Edom speaks, cannot be allowed where the flesh is taking the place of professed allegiance to God. So too the Philistine ecclesiastical assumption cannot be recognized. None of these, however, are entirely overcome. They remain in abeyance, ready to reassert themselves whenever the inevitable relaxing of fleshly rigor makes it possible.

The Philistines, indeed, continue their warfare, and Saul, whatever successes he may have had against them, was never able to check their inroads, much less to drive them from the field. But he did succeed in delivering Israel in good measure, for the time being, from their foes; and even the Amalekites, who form the subject of our next chapter, were largely subdued by him.

There was no lack of courage too on his part; and much that was excellent in administration within and conflict without, no doubt, characterized this period of his reign. We are also told, at this time, who were the members of his family and the captain of his army.

We have already learned that a list of a few names may furnish us with abundant hints as to the moral character of what is not much dwelt upon, and we might expect to find in these members of Saul's family, and those whom he gathered about him, suggestions both of the strength and the weakness which underlay his whole administration.

We may expect to find in Saul, as the first king of Israel, an intimation of what kingly rule should be; not merely what it has become in the hands of man, but, in addition to this, suggestions of what it will be in the hands of Christ. His family therefore will probably give hints of both that which is of God in government, as well as the abuse of it by man.

The names of three sons are given here, and two daughters, together with that of his wife. Jonathan, "Jehovah hath given," suggests all that is of God in this family. As the natural successor to his father, he may represent that which is of God in government, which surely always abides. It cannot, however, affect with its own God-given devotedness him who merely has the form without the reality of obedience. This explains why Jonathan, the son of Saul, acted in a way so different from his father.

Of Ishui, the next son, we have no further mention except his death, which is recorded under the name of Abinadab (1 Samuel 31:2), two or more names being often borne by the same person. "My father is willing" would suggest that he stands for but a reproduction of the characteristics of his father. Ishui, "just," or "equitable," suggests that human government when in subjection to God is a righteous thing; but, as has already been suggested, it must be in faith, or it fails to be true justice.

The third son, Melchi-shua, "My king is savior," also suggests that in true rule is safety and deliverance for the people. How little a measure there has been of that the history of Israel and of the world shows us. The true King must first come before a Savior can be known. The last syllable of his name indeed is almost identical with "Jesus," which has, however, the significant addition of "Jehovah" in the place of "king."

The daughters follow, who speak of abstract principles, rather than personal characteristics. Merab, "exalted," or "increase," speaks of that advancing greatness which is the mark of a true government; and Michal, "Who can measure?" shows its boundless extent. Both these, too, wait for their true fulfilment, not as linked with Saul, but with Him of whom it is said: "Of the increase of His government and peace there shall be no end, upon the throne of David and upon his kingdom, to order and to establish it, with judgment and with justice, from henceforth even forever."

Saul's wife, Ahinoam, "My brother is pleasure," the daughter of Ahimaaz, "My brother is strength," suggests how kingly rule has often had as its consort, not the glory of God, but that "pleasure" which will use its unlimited "strength" to secure its own ends.

Abner, the son of Ner, was the captain of his host. Abner, "the father of light," is also the son of Ner, "light"—a strange combination. One cannot be both father and son, root and fruit. As captain of Saul's army, he would suggest to us the one who upholds kingly authority and that light which is characteristic of righteous rule. "A king that sitteth in the throne of judgment scattereth away all evil with his eyes" (Proverbs 20:8). These eyes suggest the light but it must be truly that, in order to scatter away evil. The only "Father of lights" of whom Scripture speaks is quite Another than the captain of Saul's host. Well will it be for the kingdoms of this world when they are led on to victory under the glorious leadership of Him whose eyes are as a flame of fire, and whose countenance is as the sun when it shineth in its strength.

Significantly, one son is not mentioned here. Ishbosheth, "the man of shame," is the culmination of all human government. He will be found later on in the history; but here, at least at the outset, we are not reminded of the inevitable conclusion of human excellence apart from divine grace. God will allow that which is apparently good to live on unhinderedly until its own end is reached. This, alas, will be found to be in shame.

CHAPTER 12
AMALEK SPARED

1 Samuel 15

We have reached now the great turning-point in the history of king Saul. He had, as we have already seen, manifested the results of the unbelief of the flesh in failing to wait for the presence of Samuel at Gilgal, and in intruding into the priestly prerogatives, as did king Uzziah in a later day (compare 1 Samuel 13:8-10 with 2 Chronicles 26:16-21). For one under the Levitical law, an intrusion into the priesthood was a most glaring act of sacrilege. What answers to it now is the refusal of Christ in His priestly and atoning work as the only way of access to God. This will explain the terrible judgment upon Uzziah and the setting aside of Saul. No one who fails to see the absolute necessity for the sacrifice and intercessory, priestly work of Christ is fitted to lead His people. Indeed, he manifests in this act the fact that he is not a Christian himself.

It is, however, like the long-suffering of God not to visit the full consequences of one's wrong-doing upon him at once, and to grant, if it may be, a space for repentance and an opportunity for one to retrieve himself, if his former error has been a slip rather than the habit of his mind. God is not unrighteous, to confound one's being overtaken in a fault with the expression of what is his radical character. It will be found, in the day when He will judge the secrets of men, that amplest opportunity was given for men to recover themselves from any course of evil upon which they had set out. Indeed, the history of the people of God gives many illustrations of this recovering mercy.

Saul being now fully established as king, he must meet the responsibilities connected with his high office. It has been from time immemorial the bane of kings that they have used their position for themselves, their own ease or selfish ambition, rather than for serving the people. The principle, "He that is greatest among you shall be servant of all," seems to have a twofold meaning; primarily, perhaps, to show that any thought of self-importance only makes it necessary for one to be abased; but, on the other hand, the best proof of a spirit of rule, in a scene where the beloved sheep of Christ are subjected to all kinds of assaults, is to serve them; so He, the true King, could say in the fullest way, "I am among you as He that serveth."

Saul must now show his fitness for the place to which he had been called. In his case, it was the office which preceded the gift, rather than followed it. In the case of David, his fitness for the position was established in those secret conflicts which he had had, before ever the thought of rule was put before him. With Saul, he is first anointed, and must then prove his qualification.

Amalek was Israel's first foe after leaving Egypt. The Amalekites were descendants of Esau; and this, connected with the assault in the wilderness, gives us a clear clue as to what they represent. Esau, the first-born, is that which is natural as contrasted with Jacob, the younger, who suggests the sovereignty of grace which sets aside the first-born. It is the flesh which is the first-born in us, and only as born again is faith present. "The flesh lusteth against the Spirit." It may be cultivated, refined, improved, and what not, but it remains unchanged. "That which is born of the flesh is flesh." "The carnal mind is enmity against God." The descendant of Esau, Amalek, seems to suggest rather the lusts of the flesh than mere nature in general.

Referring for a moment to the assault of Amalek upon Israel in the wilderness, we find it resulted from their unbelief and doubting whether God was among them or no. "Then came Amalek and fought against Israel" (Exodus 17:8). In the book of Deuteronomy (Deuteronomy 25:17-19) we find that they were successful in assailing the weakest and hindmost of the host of Israel. This is ever the case.

The lusts of the flesh can have no power over those who are pressing forward, forgetting the things which are behind; but for those who lag, who forget their pilgrim character and become stragglers, following afar off, the lusts of the flesh have special power. It was when Peter followed at a distance that he succumbed to that cowardice which is one of the marks of the flesh.

God had commanded that when His people had entered into their inheritance in Canaan they should execute His judgment upon Amalek because of what they had done. They were to "blot out the remembrance of Amalek from under heaven. Thou shalt not forget it" (Deuteronomy 25:9). It was also declared that Israel should have war with Amalek from generation to generation (Exodus 17:16). That is, the flesh and its lusts were never to be regarded as aught but enemies; and there is to be, not surely constant conflict, but absolute hostility between the people of God and the lusts of the flesh. The time is coming, thank God, when the very name of the flesh, with all its wretched significance, shall be blotted out, so far as the beloved people of God are concerned, and become only a memory of what we once were and of a grace which has delivered us completely. This is what is before God. One, therefore, who is in the place of king—a type in that way of Christ—must be a relentless foe to Amalek. We cannot conceive of our blessed Lord sparing the flesh in its fairest form.

King Saul, alas, was himself, in spirit, an Amalekite. That is, he represented the best of what was natural. It is the one lesson of his life which stands out in prominence above all others. David and Hezekiah failed—David, more particularly. As the man after God's own heart, and one of the brightest types of Christ in the Old Testament, he was not that because of an entirely blameless life, but because he stood for the mind and purposes of God, and because, eventually, he judged all that was excellent in nature in himself, and his confidence was in God alone.

But if king Saul represents the best of the flesh, how can we expect him to be a successful warrior against it? This is manifest in what follows. It was not, of course, that Saul had any love for the Amalekites, or that he was particularly disposed to spare them. As a matter of fact, he seems to have done his work with a good degree of thoroughness. An enormous army of Israelites is gathered; significantly, the majority of them belonged to the ten tribes, there being but ten thousand men of Judah.

The Kenites, who were dwelling among the Amalekites, were warned to withdraw lest they should partake in the doom which was to fall. Then Saul seems to sweep over the major part of the territory occupied by Amalek, from Havilah close to Shur, near Egypt. It was therefore not because of any lack of power on his part, nor any sudden strength of the enemy. Agag, the king of Amalek, was taken captive, and surely the sheep and oxen offered no resistance to the victorious sword of Israel. The sparing, therefore, of the best of the cattle and bringing of Agag alive did not suggest a partial victory, but a deliberate purpose because of special desire. This is noteworthy. There is, alas, often a failure in faith to count upon God for complete victory over the lusts of the flesh. This is most reprehensible, but it is a very different thing from deliberately choosing those lusts as something to be spared.

It was the best of the possessions of the Amalekites that were thus spared. Everything that was vile was utterly rejected. How often are the grosser forms of fleshly evil unsparingly denounced and rejected while a fair show in the flesh is still being made! Thus, no one thinks of making provision doctrinally for the allowance of drunkenness and the lower vices of the flesh, yet will plead earnestly that what appeals to the aesthetic taste in ritual service, or legal formalism, or an unequal yoke with the unconverted in the work of God, may be spared and dedicated to the Lord's service. But how can that which is unclean be dedicated to Him? There is but one dedication of evil to God, and that is the dedication to the sword of judgment. The sin, therefore, of Saul and the people—for he seems to have been both their agent and co-partner in this act—was a distinct refusal to obey the command of the Lord. He had put his own interpretation upon that command, an interpretation which fell in with his own and the people's desires.

All of this disobedience God rehearses to Samuel before the prophet goes to meet Saul. God repented—not surely in the sense of having been taken by surprise at the outcome—but rather, speaking so that we may understand Saul's responsibility, which alone debarred him from the place of dignity and confidence.

Samuel is deeply grieved at this. There seems to have been a strong natural affection on the part of the prophet for Saul. No doubt he was a lovable man in many ways, and the prophet, as having been used in connection with his anointing, would feel especially the keenness of the disappointment which now is his. He cried to the Lord, perhaps pleading that fresh opportunity might be given, and that the final word might not yet be said; but with God, and indeed with every spiritual judgment, Saul's character was fully and finally manifested. Its essential was disobedience. As a matter of fact, too, he was allowed a long season in which he could have shown whether or not his repentance was genuine, and whether he could again be trusted; but the longer the space given for repentance, the more manifest is his inherent and total apostasy of heart from God.

Samuel therefore goes to meet Saul, and finds him at Gilgal, a place of blessed associations, but the scene, too, of Saul's previous failure to manifest faith. Before reaching Gilgal, he had gone to Carmel—the place of fruitfulness—and had there "set him up a place"—doubtless a memorial of some kind to celebrate his victory over Amalek. This was appropriate to one who was boasting in the excellence of the flesh and would declare his own prowess.

Saul seems (though it may be hypocrisy) delighted to meet Samuel, and apparently is ignorant of having disobeyed God. He goes out with the bold profession, "I have performed the commandment of the Lord." The prophet, who might weep in secret over the rejection of the proud king, is most faithful, however, in his dealing with him. He asks as to the spared flocks and herds, who give the lie to the king's declaration that he had obeyed the commandment of the Lord.

How often do those spared things of the flesh and its lusts contradict the bold profession of having put to death all our members which are upon earth!

Samuel now goes on to tell Saul the judgment of God upon him. There was a time when he was little in his own sight, when he shrank with greatest reluctance from any intrusion into a place of prominence. He had thus protested to Samuel on the occasion of his anointing; and later on, when declared the chosen one of the people, he had hidden himself. A change has come over him. He has become flushed with victory; he has been recognized by the mass of the people, and has attained an importance in his own eyes far different from the low thoughts he once had. Samuel recalls this past to him, and places it side by side with his present lofty disregard of the will of God.

Again Saul protests, and would seek to throw the responsibility for sparing the cattle upon the people. No doubt they were quite willing thus to spare them, but that did not relieve Saul from his responsibility as king. What king yields to his people, or obeys them? It is ever the reverse. Samuel, however, does not dispute this, or speak of it to Saul. There is another King who had given His command. It was to Him that Saul must give an account. Did He delight in sacrifices, even if all the cattle were thus to be devoted, as much as in obedience? And then follows that word so often quoted, so heart-searching: "To obey is better than sacrifice, and to hearken than the fat of rams." It tests many a specious claim to devotedness or service. How often is the plea made that we should spare something of the flesh in order to devote it to the Lord!

Thus an unscriptural course, either in the private life or in public association, is condoned on the plea that we can the better serve the Lord. The principle, "Let us do evil, that good may come," has not yet lost its power in the minds of many, and is often used as an excuse for manifest disobedience. Disobedience here too is characterized as rebellion. It is not merely neglect; it is not some trifle, for there can be no trifles in what God commands. To disobey

Him is rebellion. The first sin that came into the world was that of disobedience; and this earth has been from that day in rebellion against its rightful Lord and Owner.

The sin of rebellion is closely linked with those Satanic powers suggested in witchcraft. Indeed, Satan thus deceived our mother Eve. He led her into disobedience by his Satanic ways. How solemn and striking it is to remember that this act of disobedience and rebellion of Saul's culminates finally in that scene with which his life closes! When he consulted the witch at Endor he was linking together the beginning and the ending of his course of disobedience, and all alike had the same character of stubbornness and idolatry.

At last Saul seems to have recognized his sin; at least, there is the acknowledgment of it; but we remember how Pharaoh acknowledged his sins only to repeat them again; and how Judas, after his deliberate treachery against the Son of God, repented himself. "The sorrow of the world worketh death." It does not work repentance "that needeth not to be repented of."

He pleads his fear of the people, which, if true, showed his incapacity for all true rule. For "he that ruleth over men must be just, ruling in the fear of God;" and the fear of man is inconsistent with the fear of God. It bringeth a snare. Scripture abounds with illustrations of this. It is the bane of the life, even of many a child of God—a shrinking from the path of full surrender to Him, in the fear of what flesh can do or say.

Saul begs that Samuel will return with him, still to honor the Lord in sacrifice; but the prophet cannot compromise. The declaration of judgment had been final, and could not be retracted. Saul was a rejected man, and there must be no uncertainty as to this. Therefore the prophet, whatever his personal feelings may have been, turns away from the suppliant king. Saul lays hold of his garment to detain him, and that is rent; furnishing only an illustration that God has rent the kingdom of Israel from him, and will give it to another, a man who will answer to the thought of God. He cannot repent. God does not lightly speak here: at the very outset of Israel's history as a monarchy He must put His stamp of judgment upon that principle of confidence in the excellence of the flesh which shall abide a lesson for all time.

Again Saul pleads, not now for a reversal of the judgment, but rather that at least his own dignity may be preserved, and that he may be honored before the people. Alas, here again we see the flesh. It has its own interests, and its own honor is ever before it. It is incapable of thinking of the glory of God, and thus is branded for all time as a thing to be absolutely refused.

Samuel consents to this, as God had His own ways of working out His purposes. It was not necessary that Saul should be outwardly deposed at once. His own conduct will manifest his unfitness for his position, and therefore it could be no compromise for Samuel to return thus and worship with the king. It is, however, the last occasion in which he has intercourse with Saul. He returns to his home, ever mourning for him whom he loved, but in faithfulness never again to enter his presence. Sad and solemn parting, when he who stands for the word of God must part company from one who had proved himself to be utterly unworthy of the confidence reposed in him!

Samuel also hews Agag in pieces, as though he would illustrate God's abhorrence of the lusts of the flesh, the controlling principle of which is represented by its king. Good would it be for us if we allowed the keen sword of the word of God to do its complete work, and if we, as Samuel, would mortify our members which are upon the earth.

It is necessary and refreshing for faith to turn from one who thus utterly failed to meet his responsibilities, and who, when placed in the highest position, only showed his incompetence by disobedience, to One who never failed, and who was the contrast to king Saul in every detail. Our lessons as to Saul can be of little profit to us unless they turn us absolutely to Christ. It would do no good to know that the flesh must be refused in its fairest and most attractive forms unless we also realized that there was One who would fill the whole soul if

He is only allowed to.

Saul was in the place of exaltation when called to his service. Our Lord was in the place of lowliest humiliation when He entered upon His earthly work. Saul had a great army with which to carry out the command of God. Our Lord was all alone, forsaken even of His own disciples. But oh, how perfectly did He embody God's abhorrence of evil, and, in His work upon the cross, "utterly destroy" Amalek! The sentence of death which He bore, the judgment of God which He endured, was the complete condemnation of the flesh. The body of the flesh was put off in that true circumcision in which He marked it forever as a thing irrevocably condemned (see Colossians 2:11). It is this which makes possible also the practical putting to death, or mortifying, our members which are upon earth (Colossians 3:5). It is the crucifixion of the flesh, with its affections and lusts, spoken of in Galatians 5:24.

What marked Him at the outset was, "Lo, I come to do Thy will, O God;" at the close of His life, "I have finished the work which Thou gavest Me to do." It was at the cost of everything here that He thus accomplished that will; but in it we have our deliverance for all eternity from that which would mar heaven itself were it allowed there—the presence of the flesh and its lusts.

Any page of the Gospels would furnish illustrations of our Lord's unsparing judgment of Amalek. His dealings with the self-righteous Pharisees partly illustrate it. All that they boasted in—the best of the sheep and the cattle, which they professed to spare for the service of God—was by Him inflexibly characterized and condemned. Their religiousness, their obedience to the traditions of the fathers, their fair show in public prayer and alms-giving, were all characterized, in truth, as being absolutely rejected by God; and we can see in the sevenfold denunciation of the Pharisees (Matthew 23:13, etc.), what answers to the hewing of Agag in pieces before the Lord.

And yet He never sacrificed an iota of grace or mercy to a truly penitent sinner. Nay, one was saved who could truly characterize himself as the chief of sinners—chief because all his religious excellence which was a gain to him he found to be arrayed in bitterest enmity against the Son of God. Thank God, we need not therefore mourn for Saul, nor need we mourn that the flesh, with its affections and lusts, was so incurably evil that nothing but the sword of judgment could do for it. We turn from all vain confidences in it unto Him whose cross has judged it, and rejoice that we have as Leader and Lord one who has triumphed over it completely.

CHAPTER 13
THE MAN AFTER GOD'S OWN HEART

1 Samuel 16–17

The people's choice, king Saul, has already proved himself unworthy of the position of rule and service to which he had been called, and was therefore set aside. The act was not a public one, and so far as we know, the people as yet had no knowledge of it. With God, however, there was no thought of change. It was not the chastening of one of His children who would thus be recalled to the path of obedience, but Saul had manifested himself as unalterably unfit, because inherently disobedient. His reign indeed goes on as if nothing had occurred, except the significant absence of Samuel from the royal presence. Doubtless, this was not unusual in the sense that prophets do not usually dwell in kings' courts, and perhaps even in David's day of glory, the prophet did not constantly abide near the king. Samuel's absence, therefore, may possibly not have been known; or, if so, the people at least probably did not realize the full significance of it. Saul is allowed to go on and thus fully to manifest his unfitness.

Meanwhile, however, God calls for the man of His choice, who is one day to supersede the people's choice. This is in harmonious accord with God's ways, both with individuals and dispensations. Nations are rejected, and yet allowed, as in the case of the Amorites, to go on for years until the measure of their iniquity should be full. Individuals who have taken a final stand in rejecting Christ are not immediately cut off, but go on throughout life, surrounded still by every token of God's goodness, if they might even yet be led to repentance, though unalterably crystallized in their opposition to God. For such, in an awful sense, eternity has already begun. Well is it for us, that we do not know who such are, or when they are thus rejected. How solemn the thought: "Ephraim is joined to his idols; let him alone."

> There is a time, we know not when,
>   A point, we know not where,
> That marks the destiny of men
>   To glory or despair.

So, too, dispensationally, Israel was rejected as a vessel of testimony when the captivity to Babylon took place; yet they were restored again to their own land, and then, too, later on, came in the true Anointed of the Lord, while yet the nation as such went on, being allowed to manifest their character and to fill up the iniquity of their fathers.

So, the four Gospels give us what we have in type, the Pharisees and the nation at large fully manifested, indeed rejected as in Matthew 12, and yet allowed to go on until the final rejection of the testimony of the Holy Ghost, with Stephen. Then it is that the testimony goes out to the Gentiles, and Christ is seen to be no longer connected with the nation as such. However, judgment still lingers, and the destruction of Jerusalem did not take place until years later, when there was the final break up of Judaism, which answered to the death of king Saul.

Returning for a moment to the fact of the two natures in the believer, we have something similar to this. "That is first which is natural, and afterward that which is spiritual." The flesh we inherit, and it manifests itself; spite of every safeguard of care and testimony of mercy and truth given, it proves itself to be utterly unfit for God and is set aside. Grace then comes in and Christ is formed in the heart of the believer by faith. It would answer to the call, we might say, of David. Still, however, the flesh remains in us, no longer to be in authority, but by its presence to be a constant witness to what nature is, and how it cannot be trusted. The day is coming when its

133

very presence will be banished.

This brings us to the narrative before us. Our special subject is king Saul and to trace his course, so we must follow him on to his end, gathering the lessons his history affords and, by contrast, learn of Christ. We cannot follow the life of David, save as it is interwoven with the history of Saul. It would be a far more attractive subject, but has been so fully treated by others, that there is not the same necessity, perhaps, for going into detail.[2]

David's genealogy is given to us from the beginning. He stands out as one of the landmarks in the genealogy of our Lord, from Abraham down, as given in Matthew, or back, through His mother's line, as probably is the case in Luke, still to David and thus back to Adam. Abraham's side is given and the line of Judah singled out, and in that, Boaz continues the descent until Jesse is reached. Any examination of this genealogy would lead us too far from our subject and we must content ourselves with commending it to those who desire to prosecute that study further.

Samuel is sent to Bethlehem, the former home of Boaz, and where Jesse, the son of Obed, had his family inheritance. He shrinks from the danger involved in going thus, because Saul would hear of it and surmise his object, and the prophet seems to know instinctively that the man who is afraid of the people, still had such love for his own position that he would not shrink from putting him to death. God quiets the fears of His servant, however, by telling him to take a heifer and go to Bethlehem and say that he had come to offer sacrifice.

This has doubtless been thought to suggest a subterfuge on the part of the prophet which God commanded him to adopt, but this comes from ignoring the tremendous significance of the sacrifice and its prominent place in the mind of God. With Him, and with faith, a sacrifice meant no light matter, but that by which alone He could be

---

[2] The reader will find much profit in the "Life and Times of David" by C.H. Mackintosh; "Staff and Sceptre" by Christopher Knapp; and the full and orderly Notes in the Numerical Bible on the life of David.

truly approached. Indeed, king Saul's own anointing had been associated with a sacrificial feast. Bearing in mind that the sacrifice refers to the atoning death of Christ, our shelter from judgment, we can see its place of supremest importance.

Then, too, Samuel was not told to conceal his object, but to anoint the son of Jesse, presumably before as many as might be present at the feast. Thus, we have a beautiful type of the sheltering value of the sacrifice of Christ. Under its protection, the servant of the Lord can go forward in the very face of his enemies, knowing that all the enmity of the flesh can do nothing against that sacrifice. King Saul himself, with all his hardihood, dared not lay unholy hands upon one who had such protection.

The men of Bethlehem seem to share Samuel's thoughts as though knowing that the visit of the prophet was no idle matter, and so ask him: "Comest thou peaceably?" How our poor hearts shrink from turmoil and conflict, even when necessary, and how most would prefer the undisturbed reign of the flesh, rather than have the conflict which they fear from the presence of the Spirit striving against the flesh.

Of the anointing, we need say but little. It is a very striking repetition of the lesson in king Saul's choice. The prophet himself here is deceived when the eldest son of Jesse is presented. "Surely, the Lord's anointed is before Him." But Eliab, as Saul, is not to be chosen for the height of his stature. "The Lord seeth not as man seeth; for man looketh on the outward appearance, but the Lord looketh on the heart." All Jesse's sons are thus set aside until the youngest is sent for.

All through Scripture, we find the setting aside of the elder. Thus, Abel is accepted, while Cain is rejected. Isaac and Jacob are both younger sons; Reuben, the first-born, must be set aside, and Judah's own children illustrate the same truth that nature's excellence and the rights of primogeniture are not to be respected in the things of God. Fittingly, too, David is connected with the keeping of the sheep. A shepherd has always suggested Him who is the Shepherd of Israel, and the Good Shepherd, who giveth His life for the sheep.

When David is presented, there is an attractiveness about him which commends him. There is the glow of healthy vigor and the beauty of a countenance which expressed in some measure the beauty of the spirit within. He is anointed among his brethren, and here we see the choice of God resting upon him, marked out by the oil, a type of the Holy Spirit, even as our Lord was anointed with the Holy Ghost and with power for His work in the midst of an ungodly nation.

The Spirit comes upon David from that day, and while he resumes his lowly service of caring for the sheep, all would now have a new significance, at least in the mind of Samuel. The Spirit which had come upon David, the true anointed one, now leaves Saul, and he is afflicted with an evil spirit from the Lord. This seems to be a clearly marked case of demon possession. One who has rejected the word of God is given over to the power of Satan. It is striking that we find so many cases of demon possession in the life of our Lord, and in beautiful accord with the thought of His mastery over the demons, we see here David, His type, called in to soothe the troubled spirit of king Saul when afflicted by the demon. Of the nature of that affliction, we cannot speak minutely. Unquestionably, there was a sense of being forsaken of God, no longer having His approval. Of the utter hopelessness and despair of this, no one could speak fully. It was likely accompanied by certain clouding of the mind, or at least, such an oppression that one was rendered totally unfit for the performance of any duty.

It has sometimes been said that king Saul was afflicted with insanity. This is not the truth. Alas, it was not insanity, but the demon of evil to which he had yielded himself and which now asserts itself as his master. What a picture of him who but a little while ago was the proud victor over the hosts of Ammon, who was acclaimed with joy by the people as the man of their choice and who had the fullest privileges of the prophet's guidance, and, above all, the power of God with him! Here he is, brought so low that even his servants can only pity him. And such is the consequence of disobedience, seen here in full measure in the setting aside of one whose abilities and powers towered above all others in his time.

The servants' thought of relief is that a sweet singer should soothe the poor king in his hours of despair, and they suggest, with his approval, a man exactly suited for this. It is none other than David; and how the providence of God thus brings him into the presence of the king! There is a solemn thought that there is a kind of ministry of Christ of so soothing a character that the fears and distress of a soul may be measurably relieved without any radical cure being effected. David evidently here is a type of Christ, who by His Spirit in the ordinary ministration of His word, with its sweet tale of God's love and care, of His power too over evil, of the comfort which He brings to His own, affords solace even to those who are in their hearts estranged from God.

Our Lord while here, relieved many a case of suffering, such as the impotent man in John 5, where His mercy was not allowed to extend further because of the unbelief of the heart. There were doubtless many out of whom He cast demons, who remained still strangers in heart to Him. So, too, in the present day many in Christendom itself have been, we might say, soothed by the sweetest songs of redeeming love that have ever been heard, who yet in heart have refused the full benefit of that redemption.

Saul is attracted to David. The melody has its effect, and he is for the time relieved. He greatly loves him too, and makes him his armor-bearer, but it goes no further. He is still the proud, though rejected man, and has no thought of giving to David the place which God had given him—a place which, had he but known it, would have meant abiding peace for Saul himself.

The victory over Goliath and the Philistines, recorded in 1 Samuel 17, shows how completely unnerved Saul had become by his affliction, and how fully David was qualified to step into the place of the trembling king. It was the Philistines, enemies of Saul throughout his reign, who, spite of the victory of Jonathan, had reasserted their power, who now come up to threaten Israel.

The names of the place here are no doubt suggestive, as elsewhere. Shochoh, "His tabernacle," and Azekah, "a fence," as we might say, which protects the tabernacle. Ephes-dammim, "the boundary of blood," suggests that outcome of any struggle in which the people might engage without a God-appointed leadership. Remembering that the Philistines stand for a carnal religious establishment, and, as we have seen, representing outwardly that spirit of Pharisaic profession for which Saul himself stands, it will be seen that he had no power against them. Indeed, the lesson which is stamped upon the whole life of Saul is this. He succeeds only in the measure in which he is distinct from the enemy whom he opposes, but when that enemy is the embodiment of his own character, how could he have power against it? And this is true with all. The empty talk about self-mastery is practically the dividing of a kingdom against itself. The very conflict that confronts a Christian is the witness at least, that he is not the enemy whom he is opposing, and though he may be overwhelmed again and again, still the enemy is not himself.

The champion of the Philistines, Goliath of Gath, is a magnified Saul, where human greatness is energized by Satanic power. Goliath is said to mean "banishment." He is from Gath, "the winepress," a foreshadowing of the doom of that which arrays itself against God and His people,—banishment and treading in the winepress of His wrath, but it is this very banishment which is the weapon that strikes terror into the heart of those who are threatened by it: and Rome, to which the Philistines answer, has ever shaken this dread weapon against the trembling subjects of its authority.

Goliath's brazen armor and the number six connected with his stature and the weight of his spear's head, suggest the power of evil reaching is height as the number of the Beast in Revelation. Against such armor and such a stature, the king of Israel, who has no excellence except what belongs to him by nature, appears as a pygmy, and his armor worthless. Even Jonathan, too, here, man of faith though he is, cannot withstand the fearful assault. He evidently recognizes his own limitation and knows that if deliverance is to come, it must be by the hand of another. All here is most striking and suggestive, and the utter powerlessness of Israel to do aught, shows the complete need of a deliverer.

David's three older brothers, as we have already seen, have excellence of a character similar, but inferior, to that of king Saul itself. It is the excellence of nature. David thus comes on the scene in the glow of youth, but with no outward display of power comparable with that mighty enemy. We see in him that power which is of God, manifested in its perfection in our Lord who came in lowliness, as did David from his father with the message of love to his brethren; who seeing the enemy, goes forth to meet him in what was a real "boundary of blood" and a valley, apparently not of Elah, "mighty one," but of weakness.

He discards the armor of Saul, inferior, indeed as it was to that of Goliath, and going down into the brook, gathers five stones, the number of human weakness linked with divine power, the number too of our Lord's incarnation, God with man; and with these alone, he goes out to meet the giant foe. All victory over evil is at least a shadow of that one supreme victory which our Lord gained over the prince of this world, once and forever, at the cross. While there are details which have special reference to the character of the enemy and the nature of the victory, applicable to special periods in the history of God's people, these carry us back always to the Cross. We, therefore, would take this as the great lesson here before us.

David presents himself to Saul who, it would seem, has forgotten the one who had soothed his troubled spirit many a time before, and reassures him. The enemy was defying, not man, but God; and it was God's battle, not theirs. Thus faith ever reasons. It sees the hostile adversary not against poor puny man, but against the Lord of hosts.

To Saul's inquiry, how he could meet such a mighty foe, and he but a youth, David replies that already God has given him the victory over both the lion and the bear, and would, in like manner, deal with this foe. Our Lord had won the victory over Satan at the time of temptation, and the cross, therefore, was but the culmination of that same victory. Thus David goes forth, meets the foe, overcomes him, and a glorious triumph is the result; a triumph in which Saul himself, for the time being, shares, and David is brought before him and begins a new chapter in his life as the recognized leader of the people.

Saul himself rejoices in this victory, as though little realizing what it meant for him personally. How much the world, though dominated by the flesh, owes to the victory of Christ! The very peace and order of government are the result of that victory; and yet, alas, the world has only temporary blessing resulting from it and would cast those results away in the inevitable refusal of the reign of Christ and the adoption of the Man of Sin as their king.

CHAPTER 14
THE BREACH BETWEEN SAUL AND DAVID

1 Samuel 18–19

How beautifully does Jonathan respond to the glorious victory of David! Without a thought of jealousy or a pang of wounded pride, he strips himself of his own dignities and badges of royal authority and gives them to David, and this not in a mere outward recognition of the victory, but because his soul was knit to him and he loved him as his own soul. Well, indeed, for us is it when our hearts have been so attracted by our blessed Lord that, as the result of His victory over sin and Satan, we are constrained to strip ourselves of all that we might boast in and lay it at His feet, out of love to Himself.

Thus it was with Saul of Tarsus, who has the distinction of embodying in himself, we might say, the characteristics, before his conversion, of king Saul in all his excellence, and after he was brought to Christ, of Jonathan in all his devotion. It is grace alone that thus can change what otherwise would be a history as dark as the one that we have been considering.

Saul is quite willing that David should fight his battles, and sends him out as captain of his men of war. By the people, this leadership is gladly accepted. But how often does mere nature willingly accept the result of Christ's victory, when it brings forth from degradation and irksome bondage! It is to be feared that even God's own people forget that the Lord is something more than a warrior against their foes, and accept His service for them, while indifferent, perhaps, to His claims upon them.

David had once played with his harp for Saul, and now he would fight the battles for him, but Saul was still as far in heart from submission to God as ever he was. This comes out in what follows.

The people meet David after his victory with rejoicing. The women, with their instinctive recognition of true excellence and their simple childlike celebration of it, while giving to Saul a place of honor, set David above him. Saul has slain his thousands and David his ten thousands. Nothing could stir the heart of the self-centered man like this. Was not he king of Israel, and here they were, ascribing to David greater prowess than his own. What more could he have than the kingdom itself, and so he eyes David from that day forward.

But was it not true? Had not David slain his ten thousands? What was Saul, compared with him? Would not this reminder of the superiority of the man after God's heart have furnished an opportunity for Saul to have even yet retraced his steps and bowed to the government of God? What an act of faith it would have been; and what a lesson to the whole nation, had the king deliberately abdicated in favor of the one whom God had so signally used! But there is no thought of that in his heart. His watchful eye is upon David, and he evidently seeks occasion to rid himself of him; and yet he would still make use of the minstrelsy of David, who resumes the playing of the harp when the king is afflicted by the torture of the evil spirit.

And how blessedly our Lord Jesus shows His fitness, whether in the field of battle with our mighty foes, or in the quiet ministry of His own joy to soothe the heart. In both alike, He is supreme. There is none like Him. But Saul's enmity of David is not soothed by the ministry of his love. He throws his javelin at him to make away with him. Twice he thus seeks to take the life of his benefactor and thus confirms the enmity which possessed him. At last, he can endure the immediate presence of the sweet singer no longer, but puts him at a distance. Fearing, however, to set him completely aside, he makes him a captain over a thousand. Thus, David can continue his service of warfare and wins the hearts of multitudes of the people.

Poor Saul, we cannot but pity him. He stands in the way of his own peace, and his pride robs him of all blessing. It is ever thus when pride asserts itself. We see it in full measure in the world, but even in

142

the children of God, if pride is harbored in the heart, it thrusts out the enjoyment of the Lord, and He is, for the time, in a place of distance.

It might be thought that Saul's enmity was connected with his demon possession, but we find that his malignity pursues David with a distinct method even after he has put him at a distance from him. The original promise of his daughter as the wife of the victor over Goliath is now renewed and Saul offers her to David on condition that he will valiantly fight the Lord's battles and especially against the Philistines. The Satanic craft which marks the king here shows the true nature of his character. He will expose David to all the dangers of constant warfare and stir up the hostility of the Philistines against him by special insult, so that they shall make every effort to put him to death. Thus, while seeking immunity from the responsibility of his death, Saul is really plotting it.

Does not this remind us of the malignity of the Pharisees, who would in every way seek to entangle the Lord in His talk, so that they might alienate others from Him, and if possible, expose Him to the judgment of the Romans?

With becoming modesty, David shrinks from the dignity of being associated with the king, but fulfills all the conditions, and is eventually given Saul's second daughter as his bride. This is a very feeble foreshadow or suggestion, may we not say, of the Church which is given to our Lord, as the result of His glorious victory. "Christ loved the church and gave Himself for it."

But all Saul's machinations only gave David new occasion to show his prowess against the Philistines. So it was in the life of our Lord. The very malignity of the world, the opposition of the Pharisees, furnished the opportunity for Him to display His victorious power, and, in the face of the enemy, to let the light of His mercy and the teachings of the grace and truth of God shine forth.

Saul's enmity ripens further and now he would seek to enlist Jonathan, as well as his other servants, against him. Jonathan, however, had already given in his allegiance to David, and could not be induced to lift his hand against him. Indeed, for the time, this proves a check upon Saul's persecution. Jonathan has the opportunity of speaking well of David, of recalling his glorious victory, of reminding the king how he himself rejoiced at that time, and appealing to his sense of honor, if nothing else. Saul hearkens for the time and promises that he will spare David, who now returns to his old occupations in the king's house.

But this does not last long, the enemy still menaces, and Saul is still unchanged—a prey to the evil spirit whom he had welcomed to his heart. Again he seeks to slay David, who again escapes, even as our Lord passed through the midst of His enemies who would seek to lay hands upon Him, and goes forth, for His hour had not yet come.

David flees away. Saul shows that it was not a passing passion, but the renewal of that relentless hatred which had a definite purpose. He sends to his daughter's house, David's wife, to take David, but Michal lets him down through the window, reminding us of Paul's escape from the plotting of the Jews in Damascus (Acts 9:23-25). What a unity underlies all truth whether it be as to the enmity of the natural heart or the path of faith through the world!

Michal evidently has love for David, but it does not seem to be coupled with genuine faith here, although we would not brand her as being entirely like her father. Her act in its deception, which we do not excuse, has some points of resemblance to that of Rahab, who sent forth the spies in peace; but she does not seem to be as loyal in heart as Jonathan. However, her device shows at least her willingness to aid her husband, and he escapes in safety.

David flees to Samuel, by whom he had been anointed, as though instinctively turning to him who had the word of God which he needed for his guidance. Some are ready enough to tell Saul where he can find his fancied enemy and he pursues him there, in that relentless hatred which has now become the full expression of his character.

The similarity of the whole scene to those early days, when as yet evil had not fully mastered him, ought at least to have recalled to the madness of Saul, their brightness. Here again was a company of prophets, and here too was Samuel over them, in all the dignity of a divine mouthpiece. Saul sends messengers to take David who had found his asylum in this holy Presence, an asylum really where the Lord was his protection. The messengers succumb to the manifest power of the Spirit of God; and although the king thrice repeats his effort to reach David through others, each time they are bowed in the presence of a power mightier than that of Saul. He himself last of all comes, only however to feel afresh that to which perhaps his heart had been so long a stranger, a resistless power sweeping him along. He too prophesies, and again the old cry is raised: "Is Saul also among the prophets?"

The whole scene reminds us of that energy of the Spirit's power manifested where the people of God are truly gathered together, with no restraint upon His manifestation. It is not a speaking with tongues that dazzles; but definite prophecy, the ministry of the word of God in its appointed place, which will convict the man of the world who comes in, and "falling down, he will own that God is in you of a truth" (1 Corinthians 14:23-25).

Would that Saul had thus truly fallen down! How different a story might remain to us, for surely wherever there is repentance and the bowing to God, there is mercy and healing.

CHAPTER 15
DAVID AND JONATHAN

1 Samuel 20

As we have already seen, there is a marked contrast between Saul and his son Jonathan. Indeed, but for the relationship according to the flesh, there was nothing in common between them. Jonathan, in his initial conflict with the Philistines, in which the Lord wrought a great victory through him, and in a devotion to David which led him to strip himself of his own honors and place them at the feet of the victor, showed that faith which is the proof of a new life apart entirely from that which is born of the flesh.

Already there had been one well-nigh open breach between Saul and Jonathan which might have resulted fatally to the son, had it not been for the loyalty of the people who had delivered Jonathan from his self-righteous legal father. Jonathan, however, as son and natural successor of his father, would stand for that principle of government which is of God, and yet which, apart from divine grace, must go on deteriorating as it is handed down from father to son. This would have been impossible in the case of Jonathan, for faith does not grow old, and any measure of that is immeasurably superior to the strongest activities of nature.

Jonathan therefore occupies an anomalous position. As son of Saul, he owed him that filial respect and obedience which is the mark of every true child and which could not be arrayed against him in open rebellion. Indeed, we shall find as we go on with the history of Saul, that David himself never took up arms against him whom he always called "the Lord's anointed." It is this which is such a beautiful feature in the life of David and marks that meekness which was the foreshadow of Him who was "meek and lowly in heart."

Jonathan had already expressed in no equivocal way his attitude toward David. He had practically surrendered to him after the victory over Goliath and the Philistines, and later on, had loyally pled for him with his father, and with, as we see, temporary success. As the malignity of his father increases, Jonathan is constrained, as we shall find, to assume an attitude of devotion to David, which absolutely refuses to be identified with his persecution. It is this that we find in the chapter before us.

A further question as to Jonathan and his course confronts us at the close of what we shall now look at. Saul's enmity was so pronounced that there could no longer be the slightest question of a deliberately formed purpose to rid himself of David at all costs. David, therefore, as he had previously counted upon Jonathan's mediation, which had been temporarily successful, comes again to him, not now to seek his good offices in effecting a reconciliation which he realized to be impossible, but to bring matters to such an issue that there could be no mistake as to the enmity and the cause of it. He comes therefore to Jonathan, and asks boldly what his sin is against Saul for which he is seeking his life. Jonathan assures him that he is mistaken in this, for his father, he says, would do nothing without consulting him. David, however, reminds him of the well known devotion of Jonathan to himself which would cause the crafty Saul to keep to himself his sinister purpose.

In spite of Saul's assurance to Jonathan that David should not die, the pathetic words of the fugitive, "There is but a step between me and death," told the exact truth. So, too, it was with David's Son and Lord, as He went from place to place throughout this very land of Israel, practically a fugitive from the pursuing malignity of His enemies. His death was decreed early in His course and it was only the providence of God and His restraining hand that kept our Lord from His persecutors. There was ever "but a step" between Him and death.

When David thus appeals to Jonathan, he gets an immediate and a loyal reply. Whatever he has to propose in order to ascertain the reality of Saul's attitude, Jonathan is ready to acquiesce in. David therefore suggests a plan which will manifest everything, and while we cannot look upon it exactly as the feast to which Samuel came at Bethlehem at the time of his anointing, there are certain points of similarity. David had the right, and would naturally go to his home at the time of the feast of the new moon but there does not seem to be the same open seeking of protection against Saul as is suggested in the sacrifice which Samuel took, but rather it is used as a test to draw out what is in Saul's heart. Remembering that David is but a man, we need not seek to justify every detail here, and we must also be slow to condemn him for what was distinctly within his rights. As a matter of fact, he does not seem to have gone to his father's house at all. We therefore leave this, only calling attention to the possible feebleness of the faith which would resort to this course. We hardly think that any would feel that our Lord would have done exactly the same.

The feast of the new moon was the celebration of the beginning of a new period of time, marked, however, not by the yearly revolution of the sun, but the monthly reappearing of the moon. It is typical of the new phases of blessing for Israel; may we not see in it a suggestion that in David himself, thus anointed as king and openly separated from poor Saul, whose light indeed had been eclipsed, there was the advent of a new era for Israel? The nation still must wait for the rising, not of a moon, not of some earthly satellite, but of the Sun of Righteousness with healing in His wings, to bring in the new day for them and for the earth.

David's place, according to court etiquette, would be at the king's table, at the feast of the new moon. Should Saul miss him and inquire after him, Jonathan was instructed to resort to the ruse above described. If, then, Saul should acquiesce, all was well; but if he was enraged at it, it would be a clear indication that his motive for desiring David's presence was evil.

Having settled this, David repeats that if there is indeed iniquity in him, he does not refuse the extremest judgment that may be inflicted. Let Jonathan himself smite him. Of course, Jonathan rejects any such thought, and engages to do all that had been asked. He reminds David, too, that were there the slightest evidence of danger, he would warn him.

The next question is, how is David to find out the result of their plan to discover the mind of Saul? It would not do for him openly to return to the vicinity where there were many who doubtless would have been willing to sacrifice his life to gain favor with king Saul. For Jonathan, too, in the jealous condition of his father, to absent himself for any great length of time would have aroused suspicion. Indeed, it was a time when, with both Jonathan and David, there was the need for much care. The plan therefore is arranged—a further ruse whereby Jonathan is to go through the pretense of practicing marksmanship, and the position of the arrows, either close at hand or away off beyond the mark, is to indicate whether David can return in safety or must flee to a distance.

What has already been said as to the first plan must also apply here. There seems a certain lack of dignity about it all which may not fully consist with a strong faith, and yet we must be slow to condemn. It shows however how perilous was David's position, and how few were his helpers.

Then follows a touching scene, in which Jonathan evidently foresees the end. David must be exalted to the throne, only he pleads that when the Lord should have cut off his enemies, he would remember the covenant between them and spare his seed. How faithfully David fulfilled this pledge is seen in the beautiful history of Mephibosheth.

The new moon arrives and David's seat is vacant at the feast. Saul, with that punctiliousness of outward form which marks the Pharisee, explains his absence by the thought that he may not be ceremonially clean; but missing him the next night, he inquires of Jonathan the cause of his absence, and the plan of explanation agreed upon is carried out. Saul's jealousy and hatred at once flash out in their full malignity, blazing even against Jonathan, his heir. The fact that he is attached to David makes him for the moment hateful to Saul. The mother's name is dragged in as a rebellious woman, the cause of Jonathan's attitude. In the heat of anger he discloses the whole situation. As long as David lives, his throne is unsafe. There is nothing but the cutting off of the son of Jesse that would prevent its overthrow.

We are familiar enough with this plea in the world's history, where the blood of countless "pretenders to the throne" has been shed. Jonathan stands firm and asks why he should be put to death, and gets, as his reply, the javelin which had been aimed again and again at David. Therefore there can be no question that evil is fully determined.

According to agreement now, Jonathan goes out into the field and makes known by the sign agreed upon, that David must flee. Having shot the arrows and urged the boy who gathered them to hasten, as though he would remind David of the imminence of his danger, Jonathan sends the boy and his weapons back to the city. His affection for David will not let him leave without one more expression of it. Most touching it is. It is a time of sorrow, and only those who love as did David and Jonathan, can know the bitterness of such a separation as this; but even here David exceeds, as though to remind us that He of whom he was but a type goes infinitely beyond the love of His most devoted people.

Then the separation takes place, and David departs with the blessing of one who loved him as his own soul.

We must now ask at this point, Did Jonathan miss the path of faith here? Should he have identified himself with David and fled with him now from his father's court? Should he have reasoned, "If my father is plotting against David's life, I cannot recognize him at all and I will identify myself with David as the Lord's anointed, in complete separation from that court which it would be death for him to visit"? The question is a delicate one and involves many details. As is well known, the usual application made of it is that here Jonathan missed the path of faith and that by returning to his father's court, he refused to take the place of separation. Looking upon Saul as the implacable enemy of David and typically as representing the enmity of the Pharisees against our Lord, and further as suggesting the whole establishment of a carnal ecclesiastical system which excludes Christ, it has been thought that in Jonathan there was the one thing lacking, typical of the complete renunciation of all earthly advantage and every association with ecclesiastical assumption which is not according to God.

According to this, Jonathan stands for those who, while having received much light, and who are unquestionably children of God, devoted to the Lord Jesus Christ, do not "go forth unto Him without the camp, bearing His reproach." It must be confessed that we shrink from thus stigmatizing one of the most beautiful characters in the Old Testament, and many considerations at least should make us hesitate from too hasty or extreme a conclusion as to what would have been a better path for him than the one pursued. Most certainly, we should refuse all sympathy which the harsh spirit of criticism in any who perhaps lack much of the devotion which marked Jonathan, and yet who can lightly speak of him as disloyal or failing in true devotion to his best friend. In a day of confusion, and especially when the confusion is so wide-spread that we all are beneath its shadow, it ill becomes us lightly to characterize the tender devotion and loyalty of a true heart as being in any way like Laodiceanism.

On the other hand, David was obliged to flee. A company had already gathered around him, who shared in his rejection, profiting by his leadership, and were associated with him in his future glory; but we must remember that these were not in the place occupied by Jonathan. David himself never allowed any of his followers to lift their hand against the Lord's anointed. He was ever a sufferer, persecuted and fleeing from the malignity of Saul, but always recognizing the high office which he occupied. It reminds us to some extent of our Lord's attitude toward the Scribes and Pharisees. He said: "They sit in Moses' seat," and all therefore which they commanded and taught which was according to Moses, must be recognized. At the same time, He did not close His eyes to their own condition and walk.

David thus recognizes the position of Saul, and until the Lord's hand should remove him, he would do nothing to weaken the hold he had upon the respect of the nation. Jonathan would also have the same thoughts; and he, as the son of his father, owed that respect and obedience, may we not say, in remaining with him, to uphold him in all proper acts, while absolutely holding aloof from any evil. Thus, we may be sure Jonathan took no part in the pursuit of David. He would not have lifted his hand against his friend, and would doubtless do all in his power to hinder his evil-minded father.

It may be urged that Samuel came no more to Saul until the day of his death but Samuel was a prophet, and therefore must take the stand for God, which was called for. David continued with Saul long after Samuel had withdrawn. The whole question is a delicate one, and what should be kept inviolate in all its discussion is that in the devotion of Jonathan to David, we have a lovely example of the devotion of heart to our Lord which should mark us all.

Recurring for a moment to the application of all this to the present day of confusion and the separation of the people of God from a system of things which is contrary to His mind, we can only point out that the very devotion of Jonathan to David would lead such as have his spirit not to remain in a system which has no claims upon them, but to go forth unto Christ, without the camp. It is simply a question whether Jonathan failed in this way.

CHAPTER 16
THE PRIESTHOOD IN CONNECTION WITH DAVID AND WITH SAUL

1 Samuel 21–22

David is now an outcast and fugitive, and is entirely cut loose from any hope from the government in the hands of Saul. Instinctively, he flees first to the priest as the custodian of the sanctuary of the Lord. Apparently, the tabernacle, or a substitute for it, was here at Nob, under the care of Ahimelech, the priest. From him David would seek to get needed food for himself and his few followers. The priest, apparently aware of the disordered condition of things in king Saul's court, hesitates to aid David, but is reassured by the falsehood of the latter. A little later on, we see again the feebleness of David's faith, in feigning madness before Achish, king of the Philistines, who also drives him away.

There is no need to attempt to justify, and little occasion to entirely condemn, the course of one who was but a mere man, and hunted by a powerful and relentless foe. We can thank God that enshrined in his heart was the one purpose to glorify Him; and if we complain of the feebleness of his faith, which would lead him to resort to human expedients of deception, let us search and try our own hearts, and we may find far more of untruthfulness in them than in this beloved man after God's own heart.

The question as to his taking of the showbread has been decided for us by our Lord, who uses that apparent profanation of holy things as a sample of His own course on the Sabbath day. Everything was in confusion. Shiloh had been forsaken. The people had allowed the ark of God to be carried into captivity, and it still was without an abiding sanctuary, and therefore, in that sense, the whole priestly order, with its ceremonial requirements, was in abeyance. So too, in a far deeper way, in our Lord's day everything was in confusion; and the Jews, while professing to keep the Sabbath day, in reality, by their sin, forfeited all claim to such a holy day, and therefore could not stand for the minutia; of a ceremonial observance, questionable even in an upright people, but utterly out of place among those who were glaringly apostate from God.

Our Lord further goes on to declare His own lordship over the Sabbath, and thus completely to vindicate His course of mercy and activity of love toward the needy on the day which would have been one of complete rest had sin not entered to mar it.

David also gets from Ahimelech that which surely he had a right to—the sword of Goliath overthrown in battle. But a traitor is lurking near, who a little later will bring destruction upon the innocent priest who, unknowingly, was furnishing aid and comfort to the man whom Saul was pleased to call his enemy.

We have already alluded to David's brief stay at the court of Achish, king of Gath. He is not an attractive object as we see him, feigning madness there; but apparently his faith is restored to its simplicity immediately on leaving there, as he returns to the land of Judah and seeks refuge in the cave of Adullam. Psalm 34 shows the state of his soul after he had departed from the court of Achish. The cave of Adullam has always been connected with that place of separation with a rejected Christ which is the true abode of faith in the day of His reproach. We cannot question this; and how beautiful it is to see that here are attracted to the rejected One those whose need brings them there. It needs but little interpretation to see—in those who were debtors, and discontented, and with grievances— ourselves, who have been driven by our very needs to find our resources in One who, though rejected by man, has power to remit all debts, to heal all sorrow, and remove all discontent.

David's parents, as too old to suffer the hardships to which he was exposed, find a temporary shelter with the king of Moab. Ruth, the ancestress of David, was a Moabitess; and there seems to have been a certain measure of friendliness between David and them. Here, too, we will not too rigidly condemn him for the weakness of faith which fails to count entirely upon the faithfulness of God. Moab stands for profession; and surely profession is no place of shelter for the people of God. However, we leave this as belonging rather to a more minute examination of the character and conduct of David than it is our purpose to take up here, and pursue the less attractive subject which is before us.

But we will note that, as David had received comfort from the priesthood and affords them shelter from their enemy, so too he has the presence of the prophet of God. How good it is thus to see that if God calls his people into a path of rejection, it does not preclude them from the enjoyment of all the advantages of His presence, and communion with Him, and guidance by His word! And what was all the display that was about Saul, in array and numbers, in dignities and honors, when the prophet refused to attend him, and the priest was driven from him, while he himself was a prey to an evil spirit and his own dark heart?

Saul had heard that David had been seen, and begins at once to inquire as to his whereabouts. This shows that there was in his heart a settled purpose to destroy David, and not a mere ebullition of jealous rage which would subside. He is at Gibeah, a city of evil savor in the tribe of Benjamin, surrounded by his servants. He addresses them as Benjamites, which in all probability they were. He had been anointed as king over all Israel, and therefore his servants, from whatever tribe they may have come, would have had their tribal connection, to a certain extent, merged into the larger and more honorable distinction of serving the king of all Israel. He appeals, however, to their partizanship, and, further, to their cupidity. Would the son of Jesse, he asks, give every one of them fields and vineyards, would he exalt them to places of honor in his army, that they thus have conspired against him? He does not hesitate to drag in the faithful Jonathan too, and accuse him of having stirred up David against him. What extremes will not malignity go to in the indulgence of its mad hatred!

Do we not see here a manifestation of that enmity against God of the flesh, which He has declared? All Saul's charges were untrue. The only rebellion was in his own evil heart against God, and all his suspicions came from a guilty conscience which knew that by his own self-seeking and disobedience he had incapacitated himself for government. It was his consciousness that God had rejected him, which goaded him on to rebellion and murder, instead of leading him to acknowledge the mighty hand of God.

In response to such an appeal to self-interest, one replies, who is not a Benjamite, nor even an Israelite, but a member of the ungodly race of Edomites, the relentless enemies of the people of God. It is quite suggestive that an alien should be the chief of the shepherds of king Saul, and that the king should have as his servant one of the race closely linked with the Amalekites whom he had failed to completely destroy.

Doeg, intentionally or otherwise, misrepresents David's interview with Ahimelech. From David's characterization of it in Psalm 52, there can be little doubt that his own enmity led him deliberately to lie. Whatever would weaken the kingdom of Israel would be pleasing to an Edomite. According to his representation, Ahimelech was in the conspiracy to enthrone David. He had inquired of the Lord for him, had given him food and the sword of Goliath but even the statements which were correct were given a wrong interpretation by Doeg, and so his whole narrative was false witness, which had a most disastrous result for the priestly house.

Ahimelech and the whole priestly family are called to face Saul with his accusation. In his innocence, the priest completely denies all thought of a conspiracy. Was not David one of the most faithful of the king's servants? Had he not been sent on many a mission of importance, and succeeded in overthrowing multitudes of the king's enemies? Who then so faithful as he, and why should the priest have refused to give him that which was his right to ask? Was he not also the king's son-in-law, and did not this preclude any thought of rebellion against him? As to his inquiry of God for him, the priest utterly denies this, and the narrative shows nothing of it.

But who can alter the mind that is made up, and which sees in every one not blinded with the same hatred that marks him, or weakened with a servile compliance with his unholy wishes, an enemy that must be destroyed at all hazards? And so the priests are slain. The servants of Saul shrink from such unholy work, but Doeg is equal to the occasion, and makes good his title to association with king Saul by his slaughter of the innocent priests.

To an Israelite, this glaring sacrilege must have been a terrible revelation of the true character of the king. He who had begun by intruding into the priest's office at Gilgal, in offering a sacrifice, which he had no right to do, and who had gone on in rebellion and disobedience, now puts the seal upon the essential irreverence of his entire character by attacking God's priesthood.

Saul could spare the best of the cattle and sheep of Amalek, which he had been commanded to destroy, but his blind hatred would wipe out every vestige of the priestly family and possessions. One priest, Abiathar, escapes, and flees to David with the priestly robe. He finds his protection with the Lord's anointed, and, in the words of David, is identified with him in his danger and in the protection which his presence affords: "He that seeketh my life seeketh thy life; but with me thou shalt be in safeguard." Thus we have in miniature—may we say?—a traveling court: the king attended by the priest and the prophet and a little company of loyal supporters. What matters it that there is no royal palace—that the king must go from place to place a fugitive? God's presence is with him; and that presence, for faith, is infinitely greater than the most gorgeous palaces and the largest armies. A greater than David was attended by even fewer, and had not where to lay His head.

CHAPTER 17
SAUL'S PURSUIT OF DAVID

1 Samuel 23

We have left David in complete rejection by Saul, but thoroughly furnished, so far as was needed, for all practical communion and guidance. What more could one ask? He was the chosen of the Lord, and His anointed. He had already manifested that the Lord was present with him in both the victories gained and the deliverances from the hand of Saul. The tragic cutting off of the priests had been the occasion of the removal of this outward sign of communion with God from Saul to David, and the prophet was ready with the word in season as to his course. Thus he was thoroughly furnished unto every good work.

We find him now engaged in that work. It is remarkable to see how the proper activities of the king of Israel were now in his hands. What had been taken out of Saul's hands was committed to David. He had already been the captain of the people, and had led them on to victory; and yet he was, to the eye of sense, but a fugitive from his king, with a price upon his head, and liable at any moment to be cut off. How strange a combination, and yet how beautifully illustrative of the path of faith! For it, too, there is no outward display, no great array of wealth and power and position; but, on the other hand, the benefit of full priestly communion with God, through Christ, and all-sufficient guidance through His word and Spirit. True, the flesh is seeking ever to destroy this, but how futile it is, for it is fighting, not against man, but against God.

As we look about us today, we see the vast ecclesiastical systems of the world, from Rome on, with high pretension, with wealth and all carnal machinery for the carrying on of a great work. The mistake is often made—alas, often by the children of God—of thinking that where there is such an enormous amount of machinery, there must be power. It is this that causes men of faith sometimes to shrink from the lonely and lowly path of separation, lest they be deprived of their activity in the service of the Lord, both in ministering to His people and in the gospel to the world. It is often objected that if one gives up association with some system, it will deprive him of his usefulness. Let David speak to us here. His equipment and opportunities were ample. It was lie who was largely doing the work for Israel.

We must carefully distinguish, too, between the hostility embodied in the ecclesiastical system and the true people of God in it, together with the various endowments, or weapons, and men, which are largely at its disposal. Here too we can learn a lesson from David. He was never a reviler of the system which had cast him out. He would have been the first to deprecate a hostility on his part toward the people of God who still followed Saul. His weapons and his followers, such as they were, were at the disposal of the whole people of God to do whatever would be for their benefit. It requires devotion and absence of all self-seeking and self-righteousness to follow such a path. Indeed, no one but the One who had His Father's glory as His only object has ever exhibited, in its perfection, utter absence of all personal resentment and hostility against His relentless foes while patiently teaching them, so long as they would receive it, and ministering to the needy that were all about Him. It was the spirit which also actuated David in such good measure, and we are sure that it is that which moves the true servant of Christ, whoever and wherever he may be.

Let us cherish this spirit, and remember that, even if reviled or neglected, our great work is still to feed the flock of God, and that the words of our Master are still binding upon the love of hearts restored to Himself: "Feed My lambs;" "Shepherd My sheep."

A mere crusade against what is called "system"; a denunciation of those who follow not with us; a cultivation of a spirit of contempt

159

for them, is farthest removed from what we are looking at here. How refreshing it is when the obstacles and persecutions of the way do not interfere with the activities of divine grace working in our hearts!

We have been led to this line of thought by our present chapter, in which we find that David comes to the rescue of the city of Keilah, a part of the inheritance of Israel. The Philistines were fighting against it, and robbing the threshing-floors. David does not hastily go up to make a display of himself, as though he would show his activity unimpaired, but reverently inquires of God whether it be His will for him to go. He meets a most gracious response, and is assured that the enemy will be given into his hands. His men have not his faith, and shrink from the dangers to which they would be exposed. It reminds us of the hesitation of the disciples to return to the land of Judah at the time of Lazarus' illness. "Master, the Jews of late sought to stone Thee, and goest Thou thither again?" So David's men urge. They were afraid even where they were, and how much more if they should expose themselves to the added danger of the Philistines!

Nature ever argues thus. "There is a lion in the way; I shall be slain in the streets," is the plea of the sluggard against doing anything. But is it not true that activity is the best safeguard? To sit idly with the hands folded, to tremble because of impending evil, instead of going forward in the plain path of duty in reliance upon God, is never the way of safety. Indeed, personal safety is the last care of faith. Our present and ultimate salvation has been eternally secured, and is kept for us by our almighty risen Lord. That leaves no room for further care as to self, but rather encourages us to throw ourselves into the breach and fight manfully the battles of the Lord. Those who do this are not only victors for the Lord and His people, but themselves come out unscathed. So they go down to Keilah.

Of the spiritual significance of the place and the character of the Philistines' oppression there we cannot say much. The meaning of Keilah is given as "refuge," and the ecclesiastical system of Rome would ever seek to rob us of our true refuge. Under the plea of casting her mantle of protection over all her children, Rome actually robs them of the only true refuge, which is Christ. The Philistines were robbing the threshing-floors. As Israel gathered the golden grain, and beat it out there, these enemies would come down upon them and take away all their food.

How truly too does Rome, while professing to be a tender nursing mother, rob the people of God of their true food! The grain which is beaten out in the threshing-floor answers to the person of Christ, risen and glorified, who is apprehended by His people through the diligent study of His word and the exercise of faith. The threshing-floor would suggest the needed care and labor incident to a right apprehension of the person of our Lord. The grain must be gathered and then winnowed, in order that it may be separated from the mere empty form of the chaff, and in all its perfection offer itself for our food. The Philistines thus, in robbing Keilah, would answer to the effect of ritualism upon the people of God. It robs them of their refuge and of their food, and it is only the true David, the Lord Himself, rejected by ritualism but the chosen of God, who can rescue His people; and He does this through those instruments whom in His grace He has chosen, and who are walking in that path of faith which our Lord has marked out for us.

Thus David conquers the Philistines and takes away their cattle and rescues the men of Keilah. The victory is not merely a repulse of the enemy, but an actual gaining of fresh stores. Faith, no doubt, always gathers fresh riches from every conflict. The spoil of the enemy does not rightly belong to them, but to those who overcome them. This spoil, again, may well remind us of those fresh views of Christ which we gain from the very conflict in which we have engaged for Him.

But where is Saul in all this good work? He has not had the courage to take the initiative against the enemy. So far as he was concerned, the men of Keilah would have been at the mercy of the Philistines. Is it, however, possible that, as in the case of Jonathan, while lacking in initiative, Saul will follow in the wake made by the victorious leader? Will he not follow up the good work which David has done? Alas, he has already manifested his true character, and shown the one object which dominates him. He does fight against the Philistines throughout his reign, and yet there is one name to him more hated than the Philistines themselves, and this is none other than David, "the anointed of the Lord." What a dreadful thought! Here is a man with the full knowledge that God had chosen David, with the full knowledge also that he himself had been rejected from being king, who yet will deliberately and persistently plot his ruin. Verily this is not fighting against man, but against God.

Saul hears, doubtless through the ready tattling of the servants that were about him, that David had come to Keilah. The self-deluded king declares that God has delivered his enemy into his hand because he had shut himself up in a city, and therefore could be surrounded and besieged at leisure. The incurable character of the enmity of the flesh is seen here. Saul would not go to Keilah to deliver it from the Philistines. He will go at once to lay hold of David. What shall we say of that spirit which is timid or slothful in the work of the gospel, or in seeking to rescue the people of God from error, but which is quick to take up weapons in carnal strife with the servants of the Lord? We need not wonder that the work of God languishes in any company where the spirit of envy and strife is present.

But David has the priest with him, who will make known to him the mind of God as to his further course. It is pathetic to see that so far from the men of Keilah being stirred to gratitude by the deliverance which he had effected for them, David finds that they will deliver him into the hands of Saul, and he must therefore flee from them. So little does the average Israelite appreciate what has been done for him! And what shall we say of ourselves? Have we rightly estimated the value of that wondrous emancipation which faith has wrought for us? Do we appreciate those instruments whom the Lord has used to bring to us priceless truth which has triumphed over the Philistines, or are we ready to sacrifice to the rigid ecclesiasticism of self-will the very power which has set us free? Let us remember that a carnal ecclesiastical system would answer to Saul, and that to recognize its authority would amount to a surrender of our delivering truth into its hands.

The Lord makes known this humbling truth to David, who is thus enabled to escape from those whom he had so lately befriended. Truly the path of faith is often a lonely one, and those whom we serve we may have to leave, lest their hostility should be arrayed against us. But God is over all. His beloved servant is kept in safety to continue the work for which he had been anointed.

But though he has escaped from the hand of Saul at Keilah, his enemy still pursues him. His abode must be in the fastnesses of the wilderness, where he was well at home, and where the more cumbrous machinery of the king's army could not follow him with the same activity. It is in the wilderness of Ziph that Jonathan goes to meet David, and to strengthen his hands. It is beautiful to see this loyalty of heart on the part of Jonathan, which contrasts so completely with the enmity of his father. Jonathan reassures David he need fear nothing. The hand of Saul shall not find him. God has given him the kingdom, and he will reign over Israel. Jonathan tells David that his father knows this well—a sorrowful fact which proves his awful apostasy.

Jonathan, however, while thus encouraging David, allows his fancy to carry him further than the revelation of God. He was to have a place next to David in the kingdom. This might, indeed, seem natural. The fact that it was natural would suggest that it was not to be. In the carnal condition of the nation, it would scarcely be possible that the descendant of their former king could occupy a place next to the Lord's anointed without furnishing occasion to those who sought it to awaken discontent, and possibly rebellion. It could not be. Jonathan, under the government of God, cannot be associated with David. The natural successor of his father's throne cannot transfer his interests to a subordinate place in connection with the throne of another.

This is part of that holy government of God which we see

exercised so constantly. This world cannot be the place of final adjustment, and there must of necessity be a certain measure of reaping the consequences of one's associations where personal loyalty may be unquestioned.

We have already sought to characterize the attitude of Jonathan, and have nothing further to add here, except to remark how his soul sets to David as the needle to the pole, and to covet for ourselves that love and devotion of heart here expressed, together with the outward confession which should go with it, so far as we are concerned. Notice too, Jonathan does not return to the army of Saul to engage even in the outward pursuit of David, but to his own house. There he will remain, refusing even to seem to participate in the persecuting activities of his father.

In glaring contrast with the love of Jonathan, we have the treachery of the Ziphites. Doubtless the presence of David among them was a safeguard, but their thought is simply to "stand in" well with king Saul, and they, as the men of Keilah, show their willingness to surrender David into his enemy's hands. Saul still retains the forms of pious expression, although using them in such dreadful connection. He would call God's blessing upon these traitors because they had compassion upon him—a compassion which consisted simply in gratifying his implacable enmity; but what compassion was it for the lonely one, the chosen of God, against whom they thus arrayed themselves?

Saul urges them to find out more definitely where David is, and to bring him word. He would continue to search for him among all the thousands of Judah, and never rest until he had hunted him out of his God-given inheritance. This gives us a fresh illustration of the incurable enmity of the flesh against the spirit. There cannot be room for both to act unhinderedly in the same place. This is equally true of the individual and of a company. If the flesh is master in a man's heart, it will never rest until it has eradicated the last vestige of true faith. The same will apply to the corporate relations of God's people. If carnal wisdom and self-interest are allowed to dictate, they will root out all those blessed activities of faith which alone make life worth the living.

Saul says, "It is told me that he dealeth very subtly." Subtlety was a stranger to the character of David, save that in all the skill of practiced warfare he was an adept. This skill, however, had been shown against God's enemies, but it was a gross insult for Saul to intimate that David would use anything approaching treachery in connection with himself.

"It is told me,"—indeed! when no one knew the character or ability, and the devotion, of David better than himself! He speaks as though it were some enemy of whom he had only heard, instead of his own son-in-law who had time and again risked his life for his advantage. Can we fail to see the steady setting of the whole current of Saul's life into that ebb of all that was even naturally noble in his character, until it consummates in its awful ending?

The meaning of Ziph has been given as, "refining," suggesting that separation of the dross from the pure metal which is necessary for its full display. Here, in this crucible, Saul is but the dross, and we may be sure that the exercise of faith, dependence and patience by David would bring out the fine gold of that character which was the fruit of grace alone.

When all seems to be closing in upon David, and his capture a matter of only a few hours, the interposing hand of God is seen. Word is brought to Saul that the Philistines had invaded the land, and he has to give up his pursuit of David to go against them. This turning-point was at Sela-hammahlekoth, "the rock of divisions," a separating line indeed, which showed the presence of the true Rock who was David's hiding-place. He who had put a separation, literally "redemption," between Israel and the Egyptians, here divides between David and his enemy by His almighty presence. Thus the faith of this beloved servant of God would be encouraged by the sympathy and cheer of Jonathan, by the ineffectual efforts of Saul to reach him, and by the manifest putting forth of God's hand to protect him.

In the midst of all the experiences through which we may be called to pass, shall we not find a similar encouragement in the manifest deliverances of our gracious God? The enemy is not allowed completely to overwhelm us. We escape as a bird out of the snare of the fowler we are cheered by the sympathy and fellowship of some loving Jonathan; and when all seems at its worst, God interposes and the enemy turns away. We need not go into details, for here is the secret history of the soul, known only to God and himself but the persecuted saints of God furnish many an illustration in the pages of church history of the same character. Almost literally, as David was delivered at this time from the hands of Saul, have the Lord's suffering saints been rescued from their persecutors. The history of the covenanters in Scotland and of the people of God in Piedmont naturally occurs to us.

CHAPTER 18
THE TRIUMPH OF MAGNANIMITY

1 Samuel 24

David has opportunity, in the absence of Saul, who has gone to meet the Philistines, to remove from the threatened hiding-place of Ziph to a new asylum among the strongholds of En-gedi. When we remember that all of this took place in the wilderness of Judah, David's own tribe, it increases the pathos of his position. He had in a certain sense come unto his own, and his own had not received him. It might be added, "Even his brethren did not believe on him." This, however, is of course only speaking of him as a type of a Greater than himself.

His refuge now is En-gedi, "the fountain of the goat." The high hills are a refuge for the wild goats, and this rugged mountain tract no doubt afforded shelter for many of these climbers; and David too was like a goat—may we say, a scapegoat sent into a land cut off? But here, amid the frowning crags with their frequent caves, is the fountain still. He is not cut off from that refreshment which is here suggested. How blessed it is that the child of God, in all his conflicts and efforts to escape from the assaults of the flesh, never need depart from that up-springing well which is for him! Indeed, our Lord's own promise to the woman of Samaria reminds us that faith carries this fountain with it wherever it goes. Faith may have to leap, as it were, from crag to crag of harsh peaks, with scant footing, all the while pursued by bitter hatred, and yet it has with it the well of water springing up unto everlasting life, which insures freshness of spirit.

David at this time doubtless wrote a number of his sweetest psalms, and we can think of Psalm 63 as being the expression of his soul: "O God, Thou art my God; early will I seek Thee: my soul thirsteth for Thee, my flesh longeth for Thee in a dry and thirsty land, where no water is." No water for nature, but, as we have just been seeing, a refreshing spring for faith. In this psalm David looks back to the displays of God's power and glory as he had seen them in the sanctuary, in that quiet enjoyment, perhaps, of communion with Samuel and the prophets at Naioth, or with the priests at Nob. Those times are over, for the present at least; but even here, as he muses upon the unchanging grace of God, his soul is satisfied with marrow and fatness, and his mouth praises Him with joyful lips. He can go further; and, as he thinks of past deliverances at Keilah or in the wilderness of Ziph, he can say, "Because Thou hast been my help, therefore in the shadow of Thy wings will I rejoice." Still surrounded by evil, he adds, "My soul followeth hard after Thee." If Saul was following hard after him, he in his turn would flee all the more swiftly to Him who would not elude his longing search, but whose right hand would uphold him in the midst of sorest difficulties.

The historical setting gives significance to the closing part of the psalm we are dwelling upon. "Those that seek my soul, to destroy it, shall go into the lower parts of the earth. They shall fall by the sword: they shall be a portion for foxes." A solemn prophecy of the doom which awaited Saul! "The king," he adds, "shall rejoice in God"—not now poor Saul who had forfeited all right to the title, but himself, the anointed of Jehovah, and looking forward to the true King who shall reign in righteousness. "Every one that sweareth by Him shall glory: but the mouth of them that speak lies shall be stopped." The liar par excellence is the Antichrist, "the man of sin"—"who opposeth and exalteth himself"; and if David is a type of the true Anointed of Jehovah, so Saul has the "bad eminence" of representing the Antichrist.

Saul's campaign against the Philistines, like all his work, was of but a partial character. In fact, we do not learn of any details here, or whether there was a real clash of arms. As soon as he can turn away from the Philistines, he resumes the more congenial task to which he had set himself, of seeking David's life. And now it would seem that nothing could keep the hunted fugitive from falling into his hands.

Just here, however, where evil reaches its most triumphant height, it falls most signally before that faith whose weapons are not carnal, but mighty through God. David and his men have hidden in the recesses of one of the caves which abound in the chalk cliffs of the land; Saul himself enters the very cavern in which they have found refuge; but he was alone; and now, when the two were brought in contact, in the providence of God, it is not the triumphant host of Saul that masters the trembling flock of David, but the solitary king who puts himself in the very grasp of him whom he was calling his bitter enemy.

Here indeed is a situation, an opportunity at last, of which David's men would be quick to avail themselves. Here is now a chance for him to be rid once and for all of this unrighteous persecutor. His men even quote the words of the Lord as justifying David in taking his case into his own hands. Exactly when these words were uttered we do not know; most probably in one of the psalms to which we have already referred. David may have often repeated or sung these inspired and inspiring strains to his lonely followers in some dark hour; and now they may have turned his own words back upon himself and said, "See, the hour is come when your enemy has fallen into your hands; and shall you not now fulfill that promise of God which you yourself have made known to us—that He would overthrow him?"

What a temptation it was! And did not all seem most providential? Who would fail to justify this hunted man in delivering himself from the grasp of such hatred? We do not read, however, that there was the slightest movement on David's part to follow the advice of his men. He does, however, creep so close up to Saul that he can cut off a part of the skirt of his garment—most likely with the trusty sword he held in his hand. Even this act touches the sensitive conscience and heart of this beloved man, who would not dishonor even in this way the dignity of him whom he ever calls "the Lord's anointed."

But how easy it would have been to plunge his sword into the bosom of Saul! No such thought, however, is in his mind. Our Lord, when Judas and the officers of the law closed in upon Him in the garden of Gethsemane, showed His almighty power in that they went backward and fell to the ground. Peter, after the manner of David's men, might draw the sword and cut off, not a bit of the skirt, but the ear, only to have his holy Master disclaim any fellowship with the act. He touches the ear, and heals it. It is sweet to see the mind of the Master in the heart of His type. We may be sure it was but the anticipative fruit of a grace which our Lord has given, not to David only, but to all who follow Him.

But the little bit of the king's robe cut off by David might suggest to us the removal of the entire garment from the king who failed to wear it aright, a garment which should fall upon David. He would not now take it by force. One day, however, he would wear it in kingly dignity and righteousness; but David will wait until the time when the robe is given to him: but until then his heart would smite him even in taking the smallest portion of royal prerogative.

How beautiful are his words: "The Lord forbid that I should do this thing unto my master, the Lord's anointed, to stretch forth my hand against him, seeing he is the anointed of the Lord." Saul was still his master and the Lord's anointed, and nothing would induce David, either directly or through the instrumentality of others, to harm a hair of his head.

Little realizing where he had been, Saul arises and goes forth out of the cave, doubtless still intent upon seizing David. It is now we have a most dramatic scene, one which cannot fail to stir the coldest heart. David, who had been fleeing from Saul all this time, boldly now casts himself before him. He would heap coals of fire upon the king's head, and give him such an object-lesson of his loyalty that even the hard heart of Saul is for the moment softened. It is the self-abandonment and courage of love, which intuitively grasps the situation, and makes fullest use of it. There could scarcely be a more powerful appeal made to the heart and conscience of Saul—surely an appeal which we may well believe our gracious God permitted, who would even yet bow that proud heart in true penitence.

David lays the blame of Saul's pursuit upon others, rather than upon the king himself: "Wherefore hearest thou men's words, saying, Behold, David seeketh thy hurt?" Magnanimously he passes over the enmity so well known both to himself and to Saul, and singles out only the cowardly treachery of those who incited the king. These doubtless were sharers with him in his wickedness, although, of course, Saul was not thereby exonerated.

Had David listened to his advisers, he could have taken the life of Saul. How all this must have appealed to the proud king, and brought the blush of shame to his cheek! Touchingly, too, David addresses him as his "father," perhaps including in that title not only his kingly position as "sire"—the whole people looked upon as his family—but the more direct personal relation that existed between them. There could be no room for doubt. David held in his hand the witness that he could have slain Saul—a witness of his own integrity and of Saul's perfidy.

He now takes higher ground, and appeals his whole case to the Lord to judge between them; and goes further to speak of the solemn time of vengeance which must fall if Saul persists in his course; but David leaves it all in God's hands, illustrating that word, "Dearly beloved, avenge not yourselves; for it is written, Vengeance is Mine; I will recompense, saith the Lord." He too had been heaping coals of fire upon his enemy, and overcoming evil with good.

He also quotes a proverb, perhaps well known not only to himself, but also to Saul, who could make his own application: "Wickedness proceedeth from the wicked; but My hand shall not be upon thee." It would be hard indeed for Saul to escape from the thought that he was the wicked one from whom nothing but wickedness had as yet proceeded. David also gives him the assurance that the magnanimity already shown will be continued as long as the persecution lasts. He had committed his case into the hands of a higher power, and personally he should be pure from the blood of Saul.

He next speaks of the pitiableness of the whole scene. Here is the king of Israel, the commander of the hosts of the Lord, the anointed of God to lead His people valiantly against their enemies; and here were Philistines ever threatening the liberties of the Lord's people and the occupation of their inheritance, with other enemies ready to press in on every side; and he is concentrating all his energies upon one who, humanly speaking, is as insignificant as a dead dog or a flea. How contemptible, and well-nigh ludicrous, was it all! calculated, indeed, to stir any lingering embers of self-respect which might remain among the ashes of the desolate hearth of Saul's cold heart.

Saul seems melted and broken. What memories would that voice awaken of loyal cheer in that day of Goliath's mighty power—of gladness and hope when the dark cloud of the evil spirit pressed upon his soul—of songs of praise that told of the care of the Great Shepherd for the least of His sheep! How many a weary night had been soothed by that voice! He recalls, too, the relationship, as David had already done, possibly with the same twofold significance that we suggested there: "Is this thy voice, my son David?" and he is melted down to tears. Gracious drops indeed! Only, something more than sentiment or tender recollections is needed to melt the hard heart of pride; and what alembic can change the essential character of the flesh?

There seems to be an acknowledgment of David's righteousness, and his own sin: "Thou hast been more righteous than I." David had rewarded good for his evil. He could not deny the proofs that were before him, when even God Himself had delivered him into the hands of David. What a great moral victory for the son of Jesse! Who could deny that if an enemy falls into one's hands, he would wreak vengeance upon him, if that were really in his heart? Saul can but call down God's blessing in righteous recompense upon David for his mercy, and in that connection acknowledges that he will be king. So real is this to him that he takes occasion to elicit a promise from David that he will not cut off his house or his family name from Israel. Of this David assures him with an oath; and thus they

172

part, Saul to return to his house, and David not to his, but again to those strongholds which had thus far proved his shelter. This in itself would show that the breach had not been healed, and that David realized it would be impossible fully to trust one who had shown such perfidy in times past, and who still refused to bow to God in the whole solemn matter.

It would be well for us if we realized that a fair show of friendliness by fleshly men cannot be construed as a permanent reconciliation. The flesh and the spirit are contrary, the one to the other, and it is impossible that they should go on side by side without ever-recurring conflict. So too with those who have prominently identified themselves with evil, and who are not delivered from that which holds them in bondage. They must ever act according to the behests of their master; and while there may be temporary lulls in the conflict between the ungodly and the children of God, these by no means show a change on the part of the former.

Thus Rome has ceased its persecutions largely because it has had no power to carry them on. It would be a great mistake, however, to think that her enmity had changed, or that it was an impossibility that the fires of persecution should again be lighted. The same may be said as to the persecutions of Judaism, the hostility of the world—in fact, all that manifested itself at the cross of our Lord Jesus Christ. There, all power was arrayed against Him. His accusation was written over the cross in letters of Hebrew—the religious world; of Greek— the polite and educated world; and of Rome—the political power. All alike united in one thing—their common rejection of Christ. Since that time the world has often spoken fair to the children of God; often, indeed, it has seemed as though some of the glowing promises as to the millennial kingdom were to be fulfilled in this day. Sometimes the saints have been deceived by this soft blowing of the south wind, and have let their little craft loose upon the treacherous sea of worldly approval, only to find, a little later on, the fierce storms beating against them.

No; we can thank God when the enemy ceases to persecute, but we cannot accompany him back to his house, nor settle down at ease in the world, which is as much at enmity with Christ as ever. The stronghold is our only place until "these calamities be overpast." Let us then be ever on our guard, and await patiently that day when there shall be no need for wearing the armor, and when we can ungird the loins, and recline at the feast which celebrates the final victory over evil, and our entering into our eternal rest.

CHAPTER 19
DAVID AND ABIGAIL

1 Samuel 25

We follow now for a little the history of David, almost entirely apart from Saul. The present chapter is occupied with the interesting and profitable subject of David's experience with Nabal the Carmelite, and Abigail. We shall find here that the beloved man after God's own heart was that only by grace, and was quite as capable as others of acting in an ungenerous way, or of taking his case into his own hands.

We are first, however, introduced to a scene of mourning in which all Israel shares. Samuel dies, and the whole nation is gathered together at his funeral. Well may they lament that faithful witness who had stood for God during all those years of apostasy and the triumph of the enemy. To write the life of Samuel would be to narrate the history of the times in which he lived; for he formed a large part of those times.

How good is the memory of a faithful life! It enters into the helplessness of the nation like the strong framework of a great building which upholds and unites all the other material. His faith and example gave a stimulus to all in whom there was any heart to respond to his faithful warnings; his earnest entreaties, loyal intercessions and unfeigned sorrow were the choicest heritage of the people in the time in which he lived. No doubt he had his enemies, and the one great sorrow of his life was that the young man on whom he had set his affections, and for whom he had such bright hopes, had proved himself unworthy of the trust which God had permitted him to put into his hands. It had been his privilege to anoint Saul king. He had witnessed the acclaim of the people when the lot pointed him out as the chosen of the Lord, and had also witnessed, though he had not shared, the exultation of the people in their victory over Ammon. It had been his sad duty, however, to declare to Saul once and again his rejection by God; and, finally, he had been compelled in faithfulness to withdraw from him, and never saw him to exchange words after the great act of disobedience with regard to Amalek.

Samuel too had set David apart; and while not as intimately associated with him as he was with Saul, he no doubt followed with keen appreciation every step in his career. The people had abundant cause to remember Samuel with all reverence; and well were it for them had they, even at this date, hearkened to his solemn warnings. With them, as with their descendants of a later day, they were content rather to build the sepulchers of the prophets, to erect memorials to them in celebration of a faithfulness by which they themselves had not profited.

With Samuel, however, all is at rest. He is buried at the scene of his home labor, in Ramah, the last station of that circuit which he constantly made, going from place to place to judge Israel-Ramah, "the exalted," a fitting place of sepulture for one whose mind and heart were communing with the heavens, and whose hopes would fittingly find their fulfillment there. We do not read whether Saul attended the funeral of Samuel or not. He may have done so. It would have been eminently appropriate; but in the troublous and disjointed times in which he was living, with his own glaring inconsistencies, we cannot be sure whether he would take his place as a mourner at the bier of one who had so faithfully warned him.

The death of a prophet is a solemn event in the history of a nation. "The righteous perisheth, and no man layeth it to heart." It meant the ceasing of a voice which had always been lifted on the side of right and of God. It meant that the people were cast afresh upon God, and the question was, Would they turn to Him, or forget the teachings of the departed faithful witness?

It is not without significance that the history of David's

experience with Nabal and Abigail follows immediately after the death and burial of Samuel. Had the prophetic voice become silent in his own heart, or did he forget the admonitions of the faithful servant of God? If so, it was not, as in the case of Saul, of that permanent character which leaves no hope for repentance, but only a temporary lapse from which he was speedily recovered by the voice of prophecy, uttered, too, by an instrument whom he would little have thought of in that connection.

Nabal was a descendant of the whole-hearted Caleb, and illustrates, as many another example does, that grace is not transmitted by natural inheritance. Doubtless he had greatly profited by the faithfulness of his forefather Caleb. A fair heritage was his, and his possessions so abundant that they attracted special attention.

The names here seem significant. The general locality was the wilderness of Paran, "adornment," which, in connection with Nabal, seems to suggest an outward display which ill accorded with his spiritual condition. His home is at Maon, "a dwelling-place," suggesting perhaps the sense of security in earthly things, much like the man in Luke 12, who said, "Soul, thou hast much goods laid up for many years; take thine ease, eat, drink, and be merry." Indeed, God's answer to him, "Thou fool," is a translation of Nabal, which means, "folly." His end, too, like that of Nabal, is in solemn contrast with the luxury by which he was surrounded.

Carmel, "vineyard," would be in line with all this. On the other hand, David, though now rejected, was heir of all this as ruler of the land, and in that sense was in the midst of his own possessions— possessions, however, which he could not then enjoy, as it was the time of his rejection. It is this that makes his action inconsistent as a type of Him who, while heir of all things, abode in poverty here, and had not where to lay His head.

It was the time of sheep-shearing, when the flocks would yield up, in their fleecy wool, an enormous revenue to their owner, which he had little share in producing. It is quite significant that every action of sheep-shearing that is mentioned in the Scriptures is connected with some manifestation of evil. It was at the time of sheep-shearing that Judah fell into his grievous sin, and later on Absalom slew his brother Ammon at the feast in sheep-shearing time. Is there here any suggestion of a misuse of the flock, or may we say, at least, a failure to apprehend the fact that all blessing comes through the sacrifice? A sheep would yield its wool without giving up its life, and how many have secured outward blessings while not realizing that they were the purchase of the sacrificial death of Christ!

It seems to have been an occasion of feasting, and David would take advantage of it to replenish his scanty larder, and sends out an appeal to one who lived in affluence to remember those who had scarcely their daily bread.

While hiding in the neighborhood where Nabal kept his flocks, David and his men had not trespassed upon his rights. On the contrary, the men had acted as a wall to protect his flocks from attacks of savage beasts, and still more savage men. David thus makes a frank appeal for recognition by Nabal. Would he not give him a small portion of that which he had in such abundance?

Applying this briefly in a spiritual way, how has the world imitated Nabal in his churlish refusal of David's request! It too has its sheep-shearing, its time of gathering in rich results to which it has contributed little or nothing. It has not realized that every temporal mercy enjoyed is the purchase of the death of Christ, and that He has been their unseen protector and provider. He makes His claim—not a harsh nor an unjust one—that of their abundance they give freely to Him. We are not dwelling, of course, upon the truth of the gospel. In that, no claim is made upon the sinner. He is confronted with his guilt and lost condition, and the demand made upon him is not to offer a present, but to acknowledge his sin and to accept the gift of God. But in a general way it is true, and the world recognizes that God makes a claim upon it, righteous and equitable, which it fails to acknowledge.

Nabal refuses even the meagre pittance which David, with all courtesy, requests. Utterly unlike his illustrious forefather, so far from following with his whole heart the Lord, he refuses to give one particle in recognition of His rightful claims. Thus he establishes his moral kinship with Saul, rather than with David. His churlish reply shows how utterly he failed to recognize that everything he had was a gift from God. It was his own, to do with as he would, is all his thought; and should he take his sheep and his provision, which he had made for his servants, to give to one whom he utterly refused to acknowledge? He goes beyond the refusal to give, and adds a gratuitous insult to the one who had made the claim. "Who is David?" he says, "and who is the son of Jesse? there be many servants nowadays that break away every man from his master." To him, David was nothing but a runaway slave who had absconded from Saul, his master. Nabal probably knew something of the merits of the case. He need have been no stranger to why David was away from the court of Saul, and he himself had likely been a witness to the relentless pursuit of David. For him, therefore, to speak as he did showed more than a misapprehension. It was a willful refusal to recognize the righteous claims of one who was suffering for no wrong of his own.

We must now see wherein David missed a great opportunity of showing magnanimity toward Nabal, similar to that which he had extended to Saul. His answer to David's messengers was calculated, no doubt, to provoke any latent feeling of resentment which David may have had. It was so utterly uncalled for, so brutal, that perhaps most of us can only say we would have done what he did. But it is not a question whether his resentment was natural, but was it an expression of the faith, patience and self-denial which had so beautified his life up to this time? There can be but one answer to this. David signally failed here in his readiness to take his case into his own hands, rather than to wait only upon God.

It is but a lapse, however, as we have said, and not the bent of his heart; and God mercifully interposes to prevent His servant from wreaking a vengeance which would have remained the regret of his life. The instrument, too, chosen of God is striking—Abigail, the wife of Nabal. Often has God used the lips of a woman to recall His people back to the path of faith and obedience. Abigail acts most beautifully, and offers many suggestive hints of other truths. She does not consult with her drunken lord as to what is to be done, but quickly takes those things which David had requested, and brings them to him. When she meets him, she takes the attitude of a suppliant, and, as if she herself had committed trespass against David, confesses it. She acknowledges that her husband but answers to his name, "fool," and had acted as the fool ever does, in selfishness and utter forgetfulness of higher claims.

She would, on the other hand, assume his guilt as her own; and, with confession of that, casts herself upon the mercy of David: "Forgive the trespass of thy handmaid." Most delicately does she remind David of the danger into which he had fallen—of taking vengeance; and, as she looks forward to the time of his future kingdom, reminds him that it would be no regret, in that day, that he had not shed blood causelessly, nor avenged himself. In this connection, she goes on to own him fully as the anointed of the Lord. She recognizes that the Lord would make him a sure house in contrast to the crumbling one of Saul, or even that of Nabal. She confesses his prowess had been shown in fighting the Lord's battles, and owns, too, his innocence of all the charges made against him.

She characterizes King Saul's course in an unmistakable way. "A man is risen to pursue thee, and to seek thy soul"; and in view of all the dangers to which he had been, and was, exposed, she declares that his soul shall be bound in the bundle of life with the Lord, while his enemies will be cast away from that holy Presence. There may be an allusion, too, in the "sling" to David's victory over Goliath.

All this needs little comment. It is the full reversal of Nabal's insult, and reminds us of that confession of the thief upon the cross, who rebuked the railing of the other malefactor, confessing that "this Man hath done nothing amiss," and casting himself upon the mercy of the Lord when He shall come in His kingdom.

The cloud passes from David. Gladly does he recognize the mercy of the Lord in having spared him from the shame of his own course. Again he relinquishes his interests into the only capable Hands, and refrains from taking vengeance. A few days are sufficient to show there is never need for one to avenge himself. God smites Nabal, and in hopeless gloom his lamp of life goes out. When Abigail is thus released by death from the chain of such an alliance, David brings her into his own household, and associates her with himself. It may suggest, typically, the Church composed of those sinners who have recognized our Lord in the time of His rejection, and who, set free from the bond. age of sin, are brought into bridal relationship with the Lord in glory.

The chapter closes with another reminder of the lawlessness of Saul. He had taken his daughter Michal, whom he had given to David as wife, and given her to another. Truly the flesh tramples upon everything that is sacred, whether human or divine.

CHAPTER 20
CONTRASTS OF FAITH AND FAILURE

1 Samuel 26–27

Saul's persecution of David is resumed again after the death of Samuel. Did the removal of the faithful witness against him give occasion for the blazing out of the fires of hatred, or did his departure revive in Saul such a sense of his own dishonor and loss as stirred him up to retrieve his place, if possible, and by his own efforts set aside the irrevocable decree of God? Vain effort indeed! And yet those who are acquainted with the ways of man in the flesh know that it is one of his boasts never to accept defeat, and to struggle on in face of all odds to the end. This is what is applauded by the world, which would also justify Saul in his effort to keep the kingdom to his own family. The world also fails to see that Saul was under the judicial hand of God, and speaks of his closing years as darkened by a strange form of insanity.

Again we have the willing treachery of the Ziphites, who tell Saul of David's hiding himself in their vicinity. Both tempters and tempted are the same as in the previous case, when David escaped from Saul's hands. David seems loath to believe that Saul had again taken the field against him, but the spies whom he sends out leave no doubt about that.

Again occurs a scene very similar to the previous one. It is a beautiful illustration of the magnanimity of David, who here, however, exposes himself to far greater danger than he had done on the previous occasion.

Saul and his army are encamped for the night, and David resolves to venture down into the very midst of the camp. Abishai, the brother of Joab, one of his tried associates, volunteers to accompany

David in answer to his call. They reach the camp, find all in security, and Saul behind the ramparts, surrounded by the people, all in a deep sleep. The javelin which he had repeatedly cast at David is stuck in the earth at his head, ready to be seized at a moment's notice. Again Abishai urges David to rid himself of his enemy, offering to use Saul's own weapon against himself, with the assurance that one blow would be sufficient, as doubtless it would be. Would it not be retributive justice in slaying him with the weapon which had been aimed at David, and would it not be a fulfillment of God's word that the pit which a man digs he falls into himself?

Again David absolutely refuses to stain his hands with the blood of "the Lord's anointed." Who could be guiltless, he says, who did this? This is a marked and beautiful trait of character in David—respect for divinely constituted authority, which looks not at the character of the holder of the office, but the position which he occupies. Meanwhile he reminds Abishai that God will one day remove him, either by a stroke or his end shall come in the ordinary way, or possibly he shall fall in battle. This is sufficient for him. He will not take his case out of God's hands. He does, however, again vindicate his own integrity by indisputable proof that when his enemy had the second time fallen into his hands he has allowed him to go free.

Abishai is commanded to take the spear at Saul's head, and the cruse of water; and thus they withdraw from the slumbering camp. God himself had interposed, in casting his enemies into a deep sleep; and thus he escapes with his life from a position in which any sudden alarm would have turned the camp into a scene of wild confusion, and have ensured his destruction.

The removal of the spear and the cruse of water is suggestive. The spear speaks of the weapons of warfare, and the cruse of water of what brings refreshment. In a spiritual sense the weapons of our warfare are those of righteousness, faith and truth; and that which gives refreshment and sufficiency for conflict is the water of the word of God. Saul is deprived of both. It was fitting that the man who had set out on such a course as his should be deprived of power as well as comfort from the word of God. In every assault of self-righteousness upon Christ, in every course of unbelief and disobedience, both weapon and refreshment are removed from the one who would misuse both.

The deep sleep falling upon them suggests, too, how God causes a lethargy often to fall upon His enemies, so that they are utterly powerless to prosecute their plans against the people of God. Thus, in the history of our Lord, after the determination had been formed by the Jews to do away with Him, and when they were seeking His life, He entered with all boldness into Judea, and continued His holy work. He would go up to the feast of tabernacles, for instance, and teach in the very courts of the temple; and when the Pharisees sent officers to take Him, He continued His ministry—no man laying hands upon Him. Thus, while ministering the water of life to any that thirsted, He was also removing from these self-righteous ones the weapon they sought to use against Himself—the Word in which they professed to trust. Thus the Pharisees were left both without the spear and the water, until the time should come when they would be permitted to smite.

The same path is open to faith; and at times in a marvelous way God seems to put His hand upon the opposition which assails His servants, and gives them the opportunity of bearing such testimony as for the time being disarms the enemy.

Having removed to a safe distance, David now arouses the sleeping camp. He chides Abner for his carelessness in allowing the king to be without a guard. He taunts him, though a man of courage and having supreme authority, with allowing the king to be thus unprotected. He is worthy to die for such neglect. There could be no doubt as to the truth of David's charge, for the spear and water were witnesses of it.

Again Saul recognizes David's voice, and again repeats what is now scarcely more than mere sentiment. "Is this thy voice, my son David?" There is a ring of indignation in David's reply, and not the same tone of gentleness which marked it before. "It is my voice, my lord, O king." He challenges him to show his fault; and if he is guiltless, why does the king thus pursue his servant? He now pronounces a solemn curse upon those who are engaged in this bitter warfare. If it is the Lord who has stirred up Saul thus to persecute him, he appeals to the offering as his only shelter from divine chastisement; but if, instead of God, it is men thus persecuting him, he pronounces a solemn curse upon them, and adds that, so far as they are concerned, they have driven him out from the Lord's inheritance, and would turn him off among the heathen, to serve their gods.

This is the responsibility that faces all who would persecute the people of God, great or small. What a solemn thing it is, either by harsh treatment, cold criticism, or any other injustice, to intimidate the least of the Lord's people! It is in effect driving them out from the Lord's presence, unless His mercy comes in. "Take heed that ye offend not one of these little ones," says our Lord; for such an offender "it were better that a millstone were hanged about his neck, and he were drowned in the depths of the sea."

David's protest seems again to reach Saul, who acknowledges that he has sinned, and invites David to return. He declares that he will never more pursue him, because his life has again been spared. He characterizes his course as playing the fool, and erring exceedingly. But no confidence can be placed in the word of a man who has continually violated his most sacred obligations. So David makes no response to this, except to return the spear. Significantly, no mention is made of the water. He will put the weapon back into Saul's hands, but the Word he has deprived himself of.

Again David appeals to the Lord to render to every man his righteousness and his faithfulness. He had so acted toward Saul that he could with confidence count upon God's recognition of this. He does not ask that Saul shall spare his life, but appeals to God, who has seen his own magnanimity, to hold his life precious in his times of danger. This was an appeal he could make with all confidence; and how faithfully, up to this time, had God responded to it! No one had been allowed to touch him; and though there was but a step between him and death, God occupied that step, and none were allowed to harm him.

Saul utters one more word, the last of which we have any record which he spoke to David. Most significantly, it is a declaration of the blessing and victory which are his portion. "Thou shalt both do great things and also shalt still prevail." Prophetic words indeed! Thus from the very lips of the enemy God even exacts an unwilling tribute to his faithful servants. The promise to Philadelphia is that her enemies shall come and bow before her, and confess that she is the beloved of God. So too in the world, empty profession is often compelled to pronounce God's blessing upon the very ones whom they are persecuting, and Christians who are ignored and maltreated are declared by their enemies to be those whom God will eventually bless. In the day of final display, without doubt, the whole company of the lost, Satan and all his angels, together with those who have rejected Christ, will unite in acknowledging the blessedness of His redeemed, and their victory through the blood of the Lamb.

Saul now returns, and David goes on his way. With this fresh reminder of the almighty power of God engaged on his behalf, we would think that his faith would be greatly encouraged, and that he would continue in the simple course which he had heretofore pursued. In this he had been blessed, having been permitted to rescue some of God's people from the hands of the Philistines; but here, in God's faithful record, which never flatters His most devoted servants, we have an account of failure in David more glaring than his temporary lapse in the case of Nabal. The deliberate purpose which he forms, of dwelling among the Philistines, springs from a heart which for the time had lost sight of the all-sufficiency of God. "David said in his heart, I shall now perish one day by the hand of Saul."

How opposite is the arguing of unbelief to that of faith! Faith reasons, "Because Thou hast been my help in time past, therefore under the shadow of Thy wings I will rejoice." Every past mercy is a pledge for mercy to come. Unbelief looks upon every fresh danger as a greater menace than all that had previously occurred; and, forgetting the mercy of God, recalls only the various dangers to which it has been exposed. We need not chide David severely, but rather ask ourselves, Have not we too often fallen in the same way? The disciples also, again and again, forgot the Lord's sufficiency when we would think it would have been impossible for them to do so. He had fed the five thousand; and when the need is presented again, with four thousand to be fed, they ask the same unbelieving question. This is always nature's way. Unless our faith is in living exercise, we dishonor the Lord by doubting His care and His power. But if we lose sight of the Lord and His sufficiency, what other resource have we?

David here has no thought, apparently, of hiding in the strongholds of the land. If he loses sight of God, there is nothing better for him than to go speedily down into the land of the Philistines. But what an exchange! Those enemies against whom he had fought all these years, over whom he had won such notable victories, whose champion he had laid in the dust, he must now seek refuge with. How humiliating! Has he forgotten his previous failure when he fled to Achish, king of the Philistines, and had to feign himself a madman? And is it not mad folly to lose faith in the all-sufficiency of God, and to trust in an arm of flesh?

But we would like to get rid of the constant assaults of persecution. Without grace, we weary of oft-repeated attacks, and the soul, losing sight of the Lord, asks, Shall I not for the time being sacrifice my principles, give up my testimony, leave the ground which I see to be the heritage of God's people—can I not let all this go for the time, to secure a little ease? Here David takes the ground to which hitherto all the power of Saul had not been able to drive him. It is ever true that our greatest enemy lurks in our own hearts. Not all the malice of Satan, nor the cunning craftiness of men, can dislodge the soul which has put its unwavering trust in the living God. It is only when faith falters that a servant-maid can lead one to deny his Lord (Mark 14:66-69).

David goes, with all his household and his men of war, back to the court of Achish, to the very city of Gath where once abode Goliath. He does indeed thus rid himself of Saul but in giving up his trouble how much more does he sacrifice with it! It was told Saul that David was fled to Achish, and he sought no more again for him but it is one thing to rid ourselves of trial, and another to keep the sense of God's approval. This has already been alluded to, but we may well repeat that, whenever we are pressed to sacrifice a distinct principle and a true position, either under pressure of opposition or the plea that we shall thereby gain fresh adherents, we are practically leaving the land of Judah—"praise"—and going down into the Philistines' country.

Remembering, too, that the Philistines stand for the principle of hierarchy, and of succession—fully developed in the ecclesiastical system of Rome—we see where disloyalty to Christ may lead one.

As we have said, it was no sudden lapse in David at this time, nor is he driven away from Achish as before, but rather he asks for a permanent place where he can abide, and Ziklag is given to him. Well indeed was it for David, as it is always well for us, that Another was working for him, who would overrule even his acts of unbelief and folly. "Ziklag," we read, "pertaineth unto the kings of Judah unto this day."

David remains in the land of the Philistines a long time, a year and four months, which shows how long a course of departure from God may continue. There was, too, considerable activity at this time, an activity which it is somewhat difficult to characterize. David goes up into the land of the Geshurites and Gezrites, where also the Amalekites were, and smites them completely, leaving neither man nor woman alive, and carrying away the spoil. These seem to have been Israel's ancient enemies, and therefore under a ban, but there seems little to relieve the darkness which has gathered about David here. We cannot feel that his victory is to be classed along with those of Joshua, or even of the Judges.

Coming back to Achish, he makes a false pretense of having gone into the land of Judah, among his own brethren, with the object of leading Achish to think that he had completely turned against Israel. He has utterly cut off every one, so that none remain to give Achish the truth, who is thus led to think that David, having openly taken sides against his own people, will now be a vassal to the Philistines forever. A false position leads to falsehood, and mars even those activities which otherwise would meet with commendation. How often, too, does one seek to make up by great activity for glaring unfaithfulness. Distinct truth as to one's own place may be rejected, and a lower path adopted. Along with this may go great apparent activity in assailing certain forms of error, and a great show of faithfulness. Well is it if this show does not lead one to publicly assail those whom he knows to be in the place God would have them occupy.

The ruse succeeds with Achish, as it may succeed for a time in any case, but chastening is sure to follow. The Lord loves His servant too well to allow him to go on in a false position, and to gain prestige with his enemies by even a false declaration of his conflicts with the truth.

CHAPTER 21
SAUL AND THE WITCH OF ENDOR

1 Samuel 28

We might put as the heading of this chapter Samuel's solemn words to Saul when he had spared the spoil of Amalek in disobedience to the commandment of the Lord, "Rebellion is as the sin of witchcraft." The two parts, so widely separated in time and outward character, are really one. Well does the old proverb say, "Respice finem" ("Consider the end"). Little did Saul think, in the day when he failed to extirpate Amalek, that the spared cattle "to sacrifice unto the Lord"—in disobedience to His word—would develop into the incantations of one who had a familiar spirit. We do not realize the unity that underlies all evil; and when one link of obedience to God is cut, it means that the soul puts itself into the hands of Satan. Thus it was with our first parents. To disobey God is to listen to Satan.

Saul had been particularly zealous in seeking to eradicate those who had trafficked in familiar spirits. It is frequently the mark of a self-righteous person to have greater punctiliousness in matters of detail than the children of God. There may be two reasons for this. The Christian is at rest as to his acceptance and eternal security. The question of outward acts as merit has in that sense been eliminated. Conscience is purged, and he has boldness in the presence of God. Alas that such matchless grace as has been thus shown should be neglected, or abused; but it is a fact that the very rest of conscience, which is the believer's portion, is succeeded at times by an indifference as to matters of walk. Far be it from us to say one word that would intimate it is to be expected, or that it is unavoidable. Such is not the case. Where the love of Christ is known, it constrains the soul to walk in obedience but let divine things lose their brightness and freshness, and the very grace of God ceases to have power in the practical life.

And is there not divine wisdom in this? Is not our God so jealous that the apprehension of divine grace should be ever fresh in our souls, that He allows the outward life to show when the freshness is lost, thus recalling the soul to Himself by the very fact of its failures? It is in this sense—may we not say?—that "Moab is my washpot." God uses the workings of the flesh to bring the Christian face to face with his declension, and thus to cast him upon the Lord.

But with the legalist everything has a certain value as merit. He is seeking to accumulate a store of good works which should at last secure for him the favor of God. True, he never reaches the point where he can say he has secured that favor, and often an appearance of humility is manifested in connection with the lack of assurance, which, if traced to its true source, would be found to rest in spiritual pride. But this desire to accumulate merit to establish one's own righteousness leads to a greater punctiliousness, especially in minor matters, where no great sacrifice is involved—the tithing of mint, and rue, and anise.

This will explain Saul's activity in seeking to clear those who had familiar spirits out of the land. He would regain the favor forfeited by his failure as to Amalek through fresh zeal against spiritists—not, of course, that spiritism should have been condoned or allowed in the land, nor that a faithful king would not cut off, as David says, speaking prophetically of the true Messiah, "all wicked doers from the city of the Lord."

Everything, however, depends upon the motive from which the action springs, and God would ever recall to us the fact that it is only the good tree which produces really good fruit. Saul's action with regard to spiritists illustrates this, at one time casting them out, and at another time seeking their counsel.

The case of the Gibeonites is even clearer. Here, in an exaggerated zeal, he would break the compact into which Joshua and the princes of Israel had solemnly entered. They had made a covenant, which could not be broken, that the Gibeonites should be spared. It was, of course, self-sufficiency on the part of Israel which made them forget their need of divine guidance for every step. They were ensnared by the wiles of the Gibeonites. Yet this covenant must be respected and while the Gibeonites were made hewers of wood and drawers of water, their very presence was a reminder of a failure to seek the mind of God for everything, and a warning that, for the future, greater care should be used.

Saul, however, would ignore the solemn covenant, and act as though he were at the head of a victorious army who had just entered upon their inheritance, with no governmental limitations. He would tacitly ignore all failure, and, in figure at least, acted as those do who seek to purify fallen man to make him acceptable with God.

We are living in a day when it is the fashion to ignore the fall and proceed as though we were still in the garden of Eden. Some of us, through grace, have learned the futility of this, and the fact that the fall is a solemn reality, whose consequences must be accepted. This is what turns the heart to Christ.

As has been said, we are not condoning the presence of spiritism, but rather seeking to point out that the power which can cast out demons at any time is the power of Christ, and that one who has allied himself with Satan cannot cast him out.

The case of this woman with a familiar spirit shows the presence of the witchcraft in Palestine at this time, which had been practiced by the original inhabitants of the land. When this began we cannot say, but doubtless it has been in existence from earliest times, and has manifested itself wherever idolatry has held sway. The essence of all idolatry is the displacing of God; and where He is ignored, we may be sure that Satan exalts himself in God's place. In one sense, man is the creator of his idols; and in another, their slave; for, while an idol is nothing, it is at the same time an embodiment of Satanic power. The things which the Gentiles sacrifice, they sacrifice to devils, and not to God.

It is the practice in some quarters to mock at Satan's power, and to ignore his presence in the world; and, still more, to reject the thought of a multitude of wicked spirits; and yet we cannot read the Gospels without realizing that our Lord recognized them fully, and that their power in His day was widespread and great. In some cases the Satanic power seemed simply to manifest itself in inflicting personal injury upon the possessed one. They would be dumb, or subject to spasms, or the mouthpiece for unclean and blasphemous language. So much did these afflictions resemble insanity, that the two have been confounded. But the damsel with a spirit of divination at Philippi was not merely possessed in this way, but gave professed revelations, evidently of a Satanic character. All through the centuries the arts of divination have been practiced, in so-called Christian as well as heathen countries; and it is most significant that in these last days, when so much light and truth abound, there has been a revival, under the modern spiritualistic cult, of the witchcraft of former days. Truly man, however cultured and apparently moral, as was king Saul in many ways, is no better than his fathers. The flesh remains unchanged, and will seek those who "peep and mutter" now as well as then.

But we must return to our chapter. Samuel's death is again spoken of as if suggesting the cessation of prophetic revelation from God. As a matter of fact, this revelation had not ceased, except judicially for Saul. David still had maintained uninterrupted communication with God—though, most suggestively, we do not find him availing himself of this unspeakable privilege during the time of his sojourn in the land of the Philistines. Unbelief and communion with God do not consort together.

But for Saul the death of Samuel was a reminder of how he had been cut off from God. The Philistines, so often fought against and apparently overcome, continued to assert their power, and we find them here, at the close of Saul's reign, with undiminished strength. With Saul, on the other hand, there was a sense of weakness and a premonition of defeat which are the sure accompaniments of an evil conscience. In the hour of his terror he turns to God, not in penitence or hope, which always accompanies a true exercise, but in despair.

Long since, he had broken off all connection with God, and launched out on the broad river of self-will which was now bearing him swiftly to the final cataract. He therefore gets no answer in either of three possible ways. Dreams would be the most direct, in which God would come to him in the visions of the night, and convey His message with conviction of its truth. By Urim the mind of God was made known through the priest, in connection with the Urim and Thummim of the breastplate upon the ephod; but Saul had slain the priests, and cut himself off from that source of communication; while the prophet, the human channel of the divine messages, was dead. Thus relations are completely broken off, through personal, priestly, or prophetic channels.

A word now indicates that the initiative of seeking the woman with the familiar spirit came from Saul alone. When the evil spirit from the Lord troubled him at the beginning of his apostasy, it was his servants who suggested that a man be sought for who could charm away the gloom; but here it is Saul who asks them to find him the witch. For some reason or other, the servants are quite familiar with the location of the person desired, which shows that with all his zeal in getting rid of witches, their whereabouts was still known.

So the king disguises himself, and under the cover of night goes down with two companions to the haunt of the evil spirit, finally turning his back upon Jehovah. Thus Jeroboam's wife feigned herself to be another when she came to the prophet. What madness it is to think of God as altogether such a one as ourselves, as though He could be deceived by a disguise! The night shineth as the day to Him.

He demands that the woman shall bring up the spirit of the person with whom he desires to communicate. She, ignorant of his identity, reminds him of his own decree; but Saul undoes all his past by swearing that no guiltiness shall attach to her for what she is about to do. Thus reassured, the woman proceeds with her incantation; but here an awful surprise awaits her. Blinded and duped by Satan, the willing tool of his falsehood, she had been accustomed to receive communications from supernatural sources, but never before had such a vision appeared as that which now greeted her. At once the truth flashes upon her. The man who is seeking and the one who is sought are both before her. "Thou art Saul"; and she needs again his assurance that no punishment awaits her from him. He was, alas, in no position to inflict it. Was not he himself the instigator of her wickedness, which God solemnly thus breaks in upon

Evidently God interposes, and permits Samuel to reappear to Saul. As to details, we are not careful to ask, except that there can be no question that the prophet was personally present, and manifested himself visibly to the woman, who described him to Saul as an old man, who, he perceived, was Samuel.

God can break through the barrier which He Himself has erected when His purposes of wisdom demand it; and He can, for the time, send back one who is enjoying the bliss of communion with Himself, to give a message. But the shock given to the witch shows the exceptional character of this action on the part of God. She had been accustomed to traffic with evil spirits; but a divine messenger arising, strikes terror to her soul.

All the so-called revelations from departed spirits which are being made nowadays are, when not impostures, as many of them are, lying messages from an evil spirit with whom the medium is communicating. God does not use unholy channels for the communication of truth; and while it is quite possible for the demon to tell of various events which have taken place in one's past life, or the lives of his acquaintances, and to give "revelations" which are in accord with the habit of mind of the person who has departed, they never emanate from the departed.

This explains why such reassuring messages are returned, professedly from the spirit world, to those who are living in sin. They are assured that the departed are perfectly happy, and enjoying every pleasure, and that God is too loving to punish any, and that they can go on in their course without fear. All of this is so evidently Satanic, that it shows how the world instinctively turns to Satan for reassurance.

Quite a different message awaits King Saul. For him there is no reassurance, not even from Satan's power. Saul discloses his consciousness that Samuel must be the medium of any communication which he can expect from God, thus tacitly acknowledging his own willful madness in having rejected the warnings of that faithful servant. The king prostrates himself before one whom he had so ignored in his lifetime. The prophet asks why his repose has been disturbed from the scene "where the wicked cease from troubling and the weary are at rest," and Saul makes his hopeless plaint. The Philistines were at war with him, God had departed from him and would give him no response, and so he had in desperation turned to Samuel.

The prophet, as though indignant that there should have been the least thought that he could say aught if God refused to speak, asks, "Wherefore, then, dost thou ask of me, seeing the Lord is departed from thee and is become thine enemy?" The prophet is one who speaks for God; and surely, if the Master has no message to give, the servant has none to deliver. There is wholesome warning for us in this. Our Lord refused to continue intercourse with those who manifestly had closed their eyes to the light. Thus, when the Pharisees ask Him by what authority He does His miracles, He asks them a question which discloses their attitude toward God. What thought they of the baptism of John? Did they believe that his call to repentance was a message from God, or merely a human word? The Pharisees were not prepared to commit themselves to either horn of this dilemma. Should they declare that John was heaven's messenger, their own responsibility in refusing him was manifested; and they feared to offend the people by declaring that there was no divine element in his call. Our Lord therefore turns from them: "Neither do I tell you by what authority I do these things." In like manner He had refused to give them a sign from heaven.

When unbelievers manifestly reject the testimony of God as to their sinfulness, and deliberately are refusing to believe upon the Lord Jesus Christ, it is a great mistake for the Lord's servants to continue intercourse with them. "Go from the presence of a man when thou perceivest not in him the words of wisdom." But oh how solemn is the thought that a man may thus so effectually break off all intercourse with God that nothing further can be said to him! "Ephraim is joined to his idols; let him alone."

Samuel continues to speak. Jehovah had at last taken the case into His own hands. After all these years of patience, and with no repentance on the part of Saul, the original word which went forth is fulfilled. The language is very similar to that which had been used by the prophet years ago as Saul laid hold of his mantle and sought to detain him. As then, he declares "Jehovah hath rent the kingdom out of thy hand and given it to thy neighbor," who is now mentioned by name.

The cause too is the same—disobedience in failing to execute God's judgment upon Amalek. How solemn it is to remember that though God may long delay execution of a sentence, judgment must fall at last, and for the very sin which originally made it necessary! Indeed, sparing of Amalek is the root of all sin. God's sentence of condemnation upon sin in the flesh by the Cross of Christ declares that nothing short of its absolute extirpation will do. This we know cannot be done by any man whose only excellence consists in that which is natural. The best that could be said of Saul is that he represents human authority, "the powers that be," which are, as executors of God's judgment, declared to be ordained of Him. But mere government cannot deal with the question of the flesh. We are confronted with many illustrations of that. All the laws on the statute books against crimes of every description have failed to do more than impose a certain restraint upon the lawless. Well-meaning efforts, even of Christians, to check, for instance, the drink habit by legal enactment—how futile are human laws to this end!

Therefore the true David alone, and He by His own death upon the cross, is capable of utterly obliterating the flesh. If Amalek is spared, it means the triumph of the Philistines, not merely because one sin committed makes others possible, but be cause of the typical association of the two nations. The Philistines are but the Amalekites turned religious, with assumption of authority to impose their rule upon the people of God, answering, as we have frequently seen, in its full measure, to Rome, and wherever those principles are accepted. Therefore the Lord must leave one in the hands of a system of carnal ordinances who refuses to accept the sentence of the Cross. At last Saul has to hear the death-knell to all his former greatness. "This day" all was to be fulfilled, and Israel with himself was to be delivered into the hand of the Philistines, "and tomorrow shalt thou and thy sons be with me." This, of course, cannot mean to define the state of those who have died, but simply declares that all should be in Sheol—Hades—the place of departed spirits.

It is hardly the place here to open up the whole question of the place of departed spirits in Old Testament times. Much has been said of a questionable character, and nothing but a sober examination of the entire subject would furnish a proper statement. There can be no question that the souls of the righteous were at rest, and that the souls of the wicked were not. As to the righteous, it has been thought that they remained in an intermediate place until the resurrection of our Lord, who not only came forth from Hades Himself, but brought out a multitude of captives from a place of comparative obscurity and dread into the wondrous blessedness of what He has secured for His redeemed. There are crudities about this, to say nothing of more serious objections. The Christian naturally shrinks from the thought that Abraham, for instance, remained in a place of obscurity as a captive until the resurrection of Christ; and our Lord's mention of him in Luke 16:22-26 clearly denies this. And when we think that all blessing has been secured through the death and resurrection of our Lord, we would be under the necessity of considering that Old Testament saints did not have forgiveness, and were not born again, until after that work had been accomplished which would furnish the righteous basis on which it could be done. This we know is contrary to Scripture, and compels the conclusion that the souls of the saints in Old Testament days entered into the presence of God and were at rest in the same manner in which believers now depart "to be with Christ, which is far better." Paradise is but another name for the third heaven—God's presence (2 Corinthians 12). But we must digress from our subject no further.

When Saul hears the awful message of Samuel, he falls prostrate to the ground. That fall which had been delayed so long comes at last, and the giant tree of the forest is brought low. "The day of the Lord of hosts shall be upon every one that is proud and lofty, and upon every one that is lifted up, and he shall be brought low, and upon all the cedars of Lebanon that are high and lifted up, and upon all the oaks of Bashan…and the loftiness of man shall be put down, and the haughtiness of man shall be made low."

But what a sight—the king of Israel, the anointed of the Lord, in the house of a witch, fallen upon the earth! Well might David say, "How are the mighty fallen!" But it is not the words of a witch that have prostrated him, but the judgment of God. The outward end, however, has not yet come, and Saul must still face the foe into whose hands he put himself.

Strange ministry indeed is that of the witch, who now comes to afford him what comfort she may, which will furnish him with temporary strength to reach the army and go through the last scene. Saul would at first refuse these ministrations, apparently realizing that the end had come, and with little heart to attempt to sustain nature any further. But the counsels of the woman and his attendants prevail, and he takes the needed nourishment. But how empty it all seems! And as we think of the sinner under sentence for his sins, eking out his few days, or years, with the wrath of God abiding upon him, it is equally futile. Oh that even yet he might cast himself upon the mercy of Him who never fails the repentant soul!

The character of the food given to Saul is a mournful reminder, by way of contrast, of the feast which Abraham spread for the heavenly visitors. In their case it was the feast which faith spread, and in which God could take His part—a typical peace-offering, as the calf might suggest to us. With Saul, to receive the peace-offering at the hands of a witch would be such mockery of divine things that we cannot associate the acts together. With him it was not of faith, but unbelief; of death, not of life, of Satan, and not of God.

CHAPTER 22
DAVID WITH THE PHILISTINES

1 Samuel 29

But where, may we ask, was the man after God's own heart during this sad hour of Israel's shame? Heretofore he has been the deliverer of the people from their enemy, the champion who had gone down into the valley of Elah, taking his life in his hands and facing the whole Philistine army with nothing but his own feebleness and faith in God's almighty power. He had "slain his ten thousands" when Saul at his best had slain but thousands. Alas for man, even for the best! We find him here outwardly associated with the very enemy whom he had so often defeated. If Saul's final overthrow can be directly traced to the sparing of Amalek, David's outward association with the enemies of God can be as directly traced to his departing from the inheritance of the Lord and taking his case out of divine hands.

The chapter before us is one of many illustrations of the truth that, for the child of God as well as for the man of the world, "Whatsoever a man soweth, that shall he also reap." Let us, however, trace the story first, and then gather its manifest lessons.

The Philistines are gathered together again for war against Israel, and David is accompanying them in the rear with Achish, his special master. The Philistine princes demur to this, and insist that David must withdraw. Achish pleads that David has been faithful during his entire stay with him, but the Philistines cannot forget that this is the very one of whom it had been said, "Saul hath slain his thousands, and David his ten thousands." The princes overrule Achish, and David must depart. They pertinently ask, "What better could he do than turn over to Israel in the heat of battle, and join them in their conflict? Would not this last proof of loyalty to Saul heal any breach between them?" Achish reluctantly consents; and while assuring David of his complete confidence in him and his entire course, commands him to take his leave.

With great show of disappointment, David pleads, and uses words as to Israel which, if conscience were not entirely asleep, must have been to him most bitter. For the deliverer of Israel to speak of them as "the enemies of my lord the king" was indeed a humiliation. Achish cannot yield, even though David is as an angel of God to him; and David, rising up early, departs into the land of the Philistines, instead of going against his own people.

What would David have done had he been permitted to continue with the Philistines? Would he really have drawn his sword against the people of God and fought against the Lord's anointed, or would the anticipation of the lords of the Philistines have been fulfilled, and would they have found themselves assailed from their own ranks by David in the midst of the battle?

There seems little doubt that the latter would have been true. We can hardly think of this man of faith actually drawing his sword against Israel. They were the sheep whom he loved, for whom he had endangered his life on many a hard-fought battlefield. He knew the heart of many toward him, and, above all, he could not forget the purpose of God, both with regard to them and himself. We have seen, however, how he had put himself in an absolutely false position by leaving the land and going down to the Philistines for protection, and it might be contended that this declension had gone so far that he would even fight against his own people.

One glimpse indicates both the state of his mind and the evident purpose which he had formed. He had already gone against the Amalekites and others in the south country, put them to death, and brought back their spoil. In explaining his absence to Achish, he had declared that he had gone into the country of Judea and assailed his own brethren; and this, Achish believed. David shows that while he was so far from God that he could readily lie about his movements, he was not so lost to his responsibilities that he would actually fight against the people of God. Most likely, therefore, he had a similar plan for the present.

But what should we say of the state of soul which made such a line of action possible? How dishonoring to God, how humiliating to David, what an abuse of the confidence reposed in him by Achish king of the Philistines, was a course like this! The very fact that we are obliged to search for proofs that will exculpate him from the charge of treason is a great humiliation. When he was in the Valley of Elah, no such proofs were necessary; nor when he delivered Keilah from these Philistines; nor when, though a fugitive, he dwelt still in the country that God had given to Israel. His conduct was above reproach then, his attitude unmistakable, and therefore no explanations necessary.

Here we search in vain for any hint of God's interposing to vindicate His servant. From the narrative before us, we could not even gather whether David was for or against the Philistines. If he were brought to trial, the outward evidence would be of treason to Israel. And God will not link His holy name with gross lapses of faith and manifest departure from the path of uprightness. So far as the Old Testament is concerned, a cloud rests upon the last days of Lot, and also upon those of king Solomon. God is not at pains to declare that either of these was His own. It must be left to prayerful examination for us to gather the comforting thought from Scripture, far removed from the immediate narrative, that the one was a "righteous" man, and the other "beloved of the Lord his God." There is instruction in this of the gravest importance. God is not ashamed to be called the God of Abraham, Isaac, and Jacob but He is ashamed to be called the God of Lot.

Therefore He gives us also in this humbling narrative of David the bare facts, and leaves us to gather comfort from other Scriptures, and from the well-known character of His beloved servant. So serious is the lapse of unbelief.

What a merciful interposition it was on God's part! If David had done nothing to avoid the awful disgrace of the dilemma in which he had put himself, either to be a traitor to Israel or to Achish, God rescues His unworthy servant through the very opposition of those to whom he would ally himself. We may well believe that later on David unfeignedly blessed God for His mercy in this regard.

How often, alas, do we make it necessary that we should be rescued from our own path of unbelief by the manifest providence of God, rather than by the energy of a faith which turns to Him! We cannot censure David as though we were innocent, but seek to learn from the lesson which God has given us here that all such departure from God is a grievous dishonor to His name, and that if we are spared from the outward consequences of our own unbelief, it is not because of any faithfulness on our part, but because of Him whose mercy endureth forever.

CHAPTER 23
DAVID'S CHASTENING AND RECOVERY

1 Samuel 30

The closing scene in Saul's life must wait for its narration until God has given the record of his dealings with His poor wandering servant and restored him to communion with Himself. It is a comfort to read the chapter which is now before us in such a connection as this. It shows us the supreme importance in the mind of God of fellowship with Himself. Compared with this, the clash of nations and the overthrow of armies is a small matter. We therefore continue to follow David as he returns, apparently with reluctant steps, from the host of the Philistines.

He has been spared the humiliation and disgrace which would have attached to his character had he gone with them; but the deliverance was, as we have seen, due merely to the providence of God. It still remained for David to learn something of the bitterness of disobedience. Therefore, the chastening rod must fall upon him. "Whom the Lord loveth He chasteneth, and scourgeth every son whom He receiveth." Such chastening is a proof of God's love to His children. The world may escape the rod, but not the believer. Nor is the rod of his own choosing. If left to ourselves, who of us would deliberately select our chastening and bow ourselves to its infliction? Few indeed; and here we find that David is not consulted as to the manner in which God will bring him face to face with the consequences of his own sin.

Returning to Ziklag, David finds that the Amalekites, the enemies spared by Saul, and many of whom had been slaughtered by himself, have fallen upon his own city, burned it with fire, taken his family and those of his followers captive, with all the spoil, and made good their escape.

We read that when Israel were to go up to serve the Lord three times in the year, they could leave their defenseless homes in perfect confidence, for God had said: "Neither shall any man desire thy land when thou shalt go up to appear before the Lord thy God thrice in the year" (Exodus 34:24). But He had given no assurance that if one was in the path of disobedience, his interests would be protected. If David would associate himself with the enemies of God, in utter disregard of His interests, he need not expect that God would protect him while thus engaged, and we may be sure there was no more tender place in which he could be touched than Ziklag, where those dear to him and his followers were. The affliction which falls upon a man's household is often more keenly felt than when it would more directly assail his own person. Thus, David later on, in the death of his child, was made to feel his sin more severely than if he himself had been laid low by illness. The chastening here inflicted is multiplied in its intensity by as many men as David had, for they had likewise been robbed of all that they held dear. What a responsibility a leader has! If he goes astray, he carries with him all who follow, and involves them in the same chastening that falls upon him.

Finding Ziklag overthrown and all their possessions carried away, David and his men can do nothing but weep until they had not even strength for that. How helpless was their condition, how overwhelming their bereavement! What could they say or think of at an hour like this? Apparently for the first and only time in his history, David has to confront the vengeance of his own devoted followers. A word from him before had been enough to arrest their hand from smiting Saul. They had shared in the hardships of his rejection and had accompanied him in his exile, still faithfully yielding obedience to his every wish, but here they turn against him, and speak of wreaking vengeance upon the cause of their trouble.

It was the darkest hour in this part of the history, and just at this darkest hour we find that for which we have looked in vain during his whole stay in the Philistines' land—the outshining of the faith which we know was present in his heart. "David encouraged himself in the Lord his God." It is in the great crises of life, when all seems lost, when death indeed is imminent, and help from human resources hopeless, when those who are dearest turn against one, that faith begins to shine. It needs no congenial soil or climate in which to flourish. It is an exotic which draws its nourishment, not from the circumstances about it, nor from friends or foes, but from Him who is its only Object, the living God. And it is just here that the turning point in David's downward course is reached. From now onward, we see him marked by that faith which had led him so safely in the former years. Again he shows that it is not a vain thing to leave his case in the hands of God, and vindicates his title still to be called "the man after God's own heart."

We have probably all seen some cases of recovery. One has wandered from God and apparently been left for a time to his own devices. He may have been successful in worldly affairs, and all seems to have gone well, even though he has manifestly compromised his pilgrim character and his integrity as a man of faith. God has kept silence. Then perhaps when the shame of such a course is most glaring, the stroke has fallen. Property has been swept away, dear ones perhaps have been taken, and the afflicted man is left somewhat as Job. And now, instead of the pride and self-sufficiency and the hypocrisy which had previously marked him in his course, we find a humbled and a chastened spirit. God is turned to, and the proud soul has found in its affliction the only meeting point between a wandering saint and a holy God. Such can say with David, "It is good for me that I have been afflicted;" "before I was afflicted I went astray; but now have I kept Thy word."

The priest had accompanied David in all his wanderings, just as the believer can never lose, by his own acts, his place of access to God and the priestly intercession of our Lord. The way is ever open for him to inquire of the Lord. God always has a mind for His children and knows what is best for them when they are at their wits' end. It is faith alone that will inquire of Him. As long as there is any possibility of human effort accomplishing anything, the soul is not apt to turn to God, but here David inquires and meets with a most gracious response: "Pursue: for thou shalt surely overtake them, and without fail recover all." At once, he and his men arise and pursue after the victorious enemy. Reaching the brook Besor, two hundred, from sheer weakness, have to relinquish the pursuit, and David with the four hundred press onward. We need not be surprised if, in recovery, there are those whose feebleness of faith does not lead them onward, but this cannot hold others back. God is with His saints who have set their face to follow out His purposes and will fight for them.

Traces of the enemy are soon found, and this brings us to an interesting episode to which considerable place is given in the narrative. As soon as David's faith reasserts itself, he becomes again to a certain extent, at least, a type of our Lord. The finding of the young Egyptian and his being spared, together with the overthrow of the Amalekites, furnishes an illustration of our Lord's action, both of mercy and of judgment, to those who, on the one hand, yield to Him, or the other, are His open enemies. The young man is an Egyptian, a citizen of the world who has been a bondservant to an Amalekite. The world serves the lusts of the flesh, and how often has the servant proved it a galling bondage! When the young man falls sick and can no longer serve his master, he is discarded with heartless cruelty, and left to die. Many a poor outcast knows what this means. As long as strength and money were there, with which to serve the lusts of the flesh, they found plenty of companionship and worldly friends; but when health failed, and money was gone, they were cast off and left to die by the wayside, as the man who fell amongst the thieves.

It is here that Christ finds the fainting soul and ministers to him the consolation of His own grace and mercy. The oil and the wine, which speak of His work and the Spirit's healing, are suggested to us here in the food and water given to the Egyptian. His strength revives, he is restored, and now from being a slave to Amalek, he becomes a servant to David and leads him down to the enemy resting in careless security, and in drunken festivity celebrating their victory. David falls upon the host and makes short work of those who had robbed him of his family.

What a day will that be when the careless world who are saying "Peace and safety" will feel the blow of His sword whose grace they have despised! "Sudden destruction shall come upon them and they shall not escape," not even those who ride upon the swiftest beasts. Everything is recovered, wives, children and property, together with other spoil taken from the hand of the enemy. How completely God reverses the results of our unbelief, and how good it is to turn to Him with fullest confidence and confession of our own sin and failure.

They return now to their brethren whom they had been obliged to leave at the brook Besor, and we see how completely David's poise of soul has been recovered. The work of restoration had been complete. Selfishness and pride of heart would lead some of his followers to give their weak brethren only their immediate family, while reserving the spoil to themselves, but the largeness of David's heart knows no distinction such as these would have made, and he lays down as a policy always to be followed, that those who tarry at home are to share equally with those who have gone to the battle.

Let us not be quick to condemn these followers of David without first taking a glimpse at our own attitude toward God's people who perhaps have not had the same energy of faith—if indeed we can call it that—which we may, in some measure, have shown. Do we realize that every victory over the flesh and its lusts, every defeat of our spiritual foes, is one for the whole people of God, the results of which we are to share with them? Are we loath to minister of the precious things of Christ which we have snatched from the hand of the enemy, to those who have not had sufficient energy to recover that which is really their own? Is there a reluctance to feed the whole flock of God, and a tendency to confine our ministrations to the special few who may be more directly identified with us? These are searching questions, and our innate selfishness has too often shown itself in a certain measure of contempt, or at least refusal to recognize all the Lord's people as ours to serve. "Feed My lambs;" "Shepherd My sheep;" "Feed My sheep" has no limitation upon it, and we must not put one there. No plea that such would not make a right use of, or are unworthy of a fuller possession of the things of God, can be allowed to prevent our carrying out this ordinance of David.

On the other hand, we must guard from a careless and indiscriminate casting of the precious things of God before those who have no heart for them. Very often the best that can be given to the professed people of God, is a word for the conscience which would awaken them to their true condition and give them a sense of need. Here is where wisdom and largeness of heart are greatly needed. A mere self-righteous refusal to minister the things of God to His people savors of the counsel of David's men, which would deter him from giving the spoil to their brethren; but a loose indifference to the true claims of God is equally removed from this principle. We must remember, however, that grace predominates and is necessary for the very self-judgment which we feel is called for. Let David instruct us here.

Having restored to his companions all that they had lost, David also sends of the spoil which he had gathered to his brethren in the land of Israel. The large number of cities thus remembered shows how great had been his victory. He sends this to those who had been witnesses of his own poverty, and had, at least by their refusal to join against him, proved that they were for him. Even now, we are permitted to have a foretaste of such triumphs of our Lord, if in any little way we have shared in His reproach, to enjoy also the results of His victory; but the day for that full dividing of spoil has not yet come. What a time will it be when the least loyalty to Him, even though it has been but a cup of cold water given to one of His disciples, shall receive a recognition beyond the greatest expectation!

CHAPTER 24
THE DEATH OF SAUL AND JONATHAN

1 Samuel 31; 2 Samuel 1:1–16

We return now to Saul and follow him to the end. He went back from the fatal interview with Samuel at Endor, and with the courage of a desperation which could do nothing less, put himself for the last time at the head of his army. How solemn and awful it was! It was not even a forlorn hope, but a forgone conclusion that disaster should fall upon them. It has been said that Saul did not make the best disposition of his army, and that the Philistines occupied a commanding position from which their assaults upon the Israelites were bound to be successful. Of this we can say but little. The topography of the land may indicate that Saul had lost all judgment, and failed even to make use of the strategy which a man of the world would have seen to be best.

The spiritual truth, however, so predominates over all here, that we can leave such a question as this for others to examine. It is enough for us that disobedience here meets its governmental doom, and that the word of Samuel as to the outcome of the battle must be fulfilled, no matter what the strength of the respective armies might be. Napoleon is reported to have said that God was on the side of the heaviest batteries. Poor man, he lived to find out that God was not on his side, at last.

Few, indeed, are the details we have of the battle. Doubtless, Jonathan fought with bravery and went down with his face to the enemy. His brothers also fall, all except one, Ishbosheth, ("the man of shame,") whose very survival seemed to perpetuate the awful disgrace which fell upon the house of Saul. What a tragedy it was! Those who can appreciate a dramatic situation will find here a scene

211

more suggestive than that of Macbeth. We know not whether Saul continued to fight valiantly or not. At any rate, the battle went sore against him. We may conceive that possibly he was able to hold his own against individual assaults, and when a swordsman met him or one with a spear, possibly he could defend himself, but he was wounded of the archers who could stand at a distance, out of the reach of his hurled javelin and away from the edge of his sword. Against these, he had nothing, and was sorely wounded by them. We find later, in connection with David's lament, that he commanded to teach the children of Judah the use of the bow. Whether this, however, refers to equipment with weapons with which they could fight with the enemy at a distance, or whether it was a melody of that name, to which the lament over Saul and Jonathan was set, we cannot speak certainly. In either case, it is suggestive that reference is probably made to the means by which Saul was wounded.

He did not, however, meet his death by the arrow. He was wounded sorely, or as it may be rendered, "writhed sore because of the archers" and knew that his fighting was over. Under these circumstances, he calls to his armor-bearer to put him out of his misery. This, apparently with some sense of what was due to God and to the high office which Saul held, the armor-bearer refused to do. But when we compare this armor-bearer with the one who so courageously followed Jonathan, when single handed they faced the whole Philistine army, what a fall we have! All that he does is to imitate Saul in his suicide.

We must note, however, one expression which falls from Saul with regard to the Philistines. He begged his armor-bearer to put him to death "lest these uncircumcised come and thrust me through and abuse me." Was there the faintest shadow of faith in this expression? Did he still draw a distinction between himself and the uncircumcised, those who had no mark of the divine covenant upon them? Faint indeed is the glimmer, so faint that we cannot connect any faith with it. The expression might well be used by one who would speak thus of his enemies, and his evident solicitude is that his person may not be subjected to the humiliation of captivity and mutilation.

Self-righteousness will preserve its reputation to the very last, and seek to guard itself from the humiliation of a public exposure of that which it would fain hide. Pride cleaves to the last to poor Saul, and he who had pled with Samuel to remain and honor him before the people, now would seek to guard the last vestiges of that honor, which he had already sacrificed by his disobedience, from further degradation. What then is to be his resource? Will he, even when thus sorely wounded by the archers, turn to God and throw himself upon His mercy? Will he thus prove that though the archers have sorely shot at him and wounded him, his hands are made strong by the mighty One of Jacob? Alas, in this hour of hopeless distress, he does not turn to God. His own sword with which he had been meeting the enemy, a figure, we may say, of the sword of the Spirit which is the word of God, he turns against his own bosom and falls upon it. He thus becomes the first suicide of whom we have a definite record in Scripture. He comes to his end, so far as his responsibility is concerned, by his own hand. What solemn food for meditation is here!

Disobedience, or refusal to make a full end of the flesh, specious though the excuses for not doing so may be, ends in self-destruction. Sin is suicide. In what dreadful company does this act of self-destruction put king Saul! He is with Ahithophel, the traitor who, like himself, sought the life of David, and is associated also with that still darker traitor who sold his Lord and then, in hopeless remorse, went out and hanged himself. Dark indeed is the scene about mount Gilboa. We would not tarry there from choice. One of the high places of Israel, it is a scene of crowning dishonor, but we must linger a while longer, in order to gather further lessons of the exceeding sinfulness of sin and the utter futility of the flesh.

It seems that even in his own act of self-destruction, king Saul was not entirely successful. Passing over for a moment to the next chapter, in the Amalekite's account to David, we find that he was still leaning upon his spear when he passed that way, and it was again at his request that this stranger finally slew Saul. Thus, three times did he show the deliberate purpose that he would not fall alive into the hand of the Philistines. Three times was he a responsible suicide: once when he besought his armor-bearer to slay him; the second time when he fell upon his own sword; and the third time when he made the final request of the Amalekite. There can be no doubt, then, of his purpose.

It was an Amalekite that slew Saul, suggesting what we have already seen, that sin is self-destruction: one of the very nation which he had failed to completely destroy now rises up to make an end of him. Truly, God's ways are equal; He links thus for us the beginning and the ending of sin. A spared Amalekite—some lust of the flesh pandered to and allowed, harmless it may seem in itself, but a deliberate sparing of evil opens the way for this closing act of shame; the spared sin, we may say, rises up to complete the work of self-destruction.

At last, Saul and his sons are dead; and now on that shameful field of Gilboa, we see the Philistine ghouls appear to rob the bodies and expose them to all indignity. The poor, dismembered body, stripped of its armor which is carried as a trophy and put in the house of Ashtoreth, is nailed against the walls of Bethshan, "the house of quiet"—what a quiet! not that which is from Him who "giveth His beloved sleep." The Philistines are apparently oblivious of how their previous victory had been followed by disaster, when they gave the glory of it to Dagon, their god. They bring the head of Saul into the house of Dagon, and his armor into the house of their goddess Ashtoreth. A female deity had prevailed over the pride of Israel, and by implication, in their minds at least, over Jehovah Himself.

One gleam of light shines in at the close of this dark story, which recalls the brightest page in poor Saul's life—his victory over Ammon, by which he rescued the men of Jabesh Gilead (1 Samuel 11). Evidently in remembrance of this, these now come by night and take the bodies of Saul and his sons from the walls of Bethshan, bring them to Jabesh, and burn them and mourn for seven days. It was appropriate that they should do this, and is in accord with that spirit of loyalty which recognizes whatever it can, even in the life of those whose main course has been evil.

We recur now to David, who has returned from a far different conflict, in which he has overthrown the Amalekites. The young man who claimed to have made way with Saul, takes his crown and his bracelet and brings them to David. He evidently thinks that he is the bearer of good tidings, and that the news he brings, with the proof of its truth in the crown and signet, will win for him some special reward and possible dignity at the hands of David. He could have no other thought than that it would be an occasion of rejoicing. He tells, with apparent truthfulness, and possibly boasting, of his share in the death of Saul, only to find that his news is met with mourning. The sorrow is first prominent. With rent garments and fasting, David and his men deplore the disaster: "And they mourned, and wept, and fasted until even, for Saul and for Jonathan his son, and for the people of the Lord, and for the house of Israel; because they were fallen by the sword."

David now asks the young man who had brought the news, whence he was, and then the stern question is put to him: "How wast thou not afraid to stretch forth thy hand to destroy the Lord's anointed?" The very first act, we may say, of David, after what we may call his accession, is thus to inflict retribution upon the Amalekite. It was fitting that he should do so. It showed his entire refusal of any share in the taking away of his longtime adversary. It was to be the Lord's hand alone, and not his own, which would rid him of the oppressor. His reverence for the kingly authority, and his recognition that Saul, with all his folly, was the Lord's anointed, are thus maintained by him in putting to death one who would desecrate him.

The victory of the Philistines is, for the time being, complete. The terrified Israelites leave their homes, and their cities to the conquerors, who dwell in them. Every defeat by the enemy becomes

215

thus an occupation of territory which should belong to the people of God.

We find in 1 Chronicles 10, a parallel narrative of the death of Saul, largely identical with that in Samuel. The conclusion, however, after the manner of Chronicles, gives the reason for what had happened: "So Saul died for his transgressions which he committed against the Lord, even against the word of the Lord which he kept not, and also for asking counsel of one that had a familiar spirit, to inquire of it; and inquired not of the Lord: therefore, He slew him and turned the kingdom unto David, the son of Jesse."

It will thus be seen that the death of Saul was consequent, not only upon his original act of disobedience, but the confirmation of his whole course of unbelief and departure from God which culminated in his seeking the witch at Endor, instead of inquiring of the Lord. It shows us that even at the very last, he might have turned to Him whom he had so deeply dishonored. How much better it would have been had he died, saying with Job: "Though he slay me, yet will I trust;" or with Esther, "If I perish, I perish."

CHAPTER 25
DAVID'S LAMENT OVER SAUL AND JONATHAN

2 Samuel 1: 17–27

By the death of Saul, all barriers to the accession of David to the throne were removed; at least, all which David was in any way bound to recognize. There are, no doubt, deeply important typical lessons to be gathered from the passing of the crown from the house of Saul to the son of Jesse. We have already dwelt upon that which is largely personal in the life of Saul, as representing the excellence of the flesh in its best form. We need not repeat these lessons here, save to remember that they should be indelibly written upon our hearts.

It is a fact that this man of the flesh is put upon the throne. That gives us another typical lesson of great importance. His kingly authority suggests the setting up of those "powers that be," of government, which God has established. There can be no question of this in our mind and it is ever the mark of an obedient Christian to recognize this authority, fearing its judgment, and deserving its praise (Romans 13:1-8). Since the days of Noah, God has established government upon the earth. It is suggestive that when He called out His people Israel to be a peculiar nation for Himself, he did not set a king over them, but showed that His own government was that under which they ought to have rejoiced. They desire, however, a king like all the nations, and their choice is given to them: "I gave them a king in Mine anger and took him away in My wrath." That is, God would teach men that governmental authority must finally rest in His hands —the hands of Him who is "God manifest in the flesh."

In the history of Saul, therefore, we may say we have the history of human government and kingly authority under its most favorable aspects, so far as man is concerned. The end, we have seen, is self-destruction. The whole course of prophetic history as outlined in the book of Daniel, confirms all this, while the New Testament reiterates the same solemn lesson. God must "overturn, overturn, overturn," all power "until He come whose right it is." We find therefore in the setting aside of Saul, typically the setting aside of mere human government. Christ is the only One upon whose shoulders the government can be placed and rest securely. He whose name is "Wonderful, Counselor, the Mighty God," is also the "Father of Eternity" and will finally, in His own blessed person, merge the millennial kingdom of the Son of Man, where evil is kept in restraint, into that eternal state where government ceases to have the character of restraint and passes into the wider, deeper, fuller and therefore the eternal fact that God is "all in all."

We have, in the passing of Saul, the close typically of human government committed to the hands of man. Prophecy furnishes many details of judgment, of which, perhaps, the wars of David with his enemies are the type; but in the accession of the son of Jesse, we have the foreshadow of that kingdom which rests in the hands of One who will never fail.

Bearing these two thoughts in mind, the refusal of the flesh and the setting aside of human government we have in David's lament over Saul and Jonathan, a most fitting and exquisite close to the sad life whose course we have been tracing. Personally, nothing could be more lovely than that David should put the crown upon the course of his own forbearance and lowliness in thus laying a wreath upon the grave of his bitter enemy. It was no formal act, no perfunctory or official threnody which he composed, but the outpouring of a tender and faithful heart which showed even at this time the love which he had evidently had for poor Saul throughout his entire history. Nowhere does the character of David shine out more clearly than it does in the subdued light of this elegy. Unselfishness, the ignoring of Saul's evil, the entire absence of personal resentment and of the slightest note of triumph, all are here present. The love, too, for Jonathan, deeper and sweeter than could possibly be had for Saul, finds here fitting expression. The very brevity of the elegy shows all the more its beauty.

But we remember that David is a type of his Son and Lord, and this reminds us of a deeper sorrow than that felt by the son of Jesse. When we think how our Lord looked, for instance, upon the young man who turned away from Him because he had great possessions; when we see Him as He beheld the city which was so soon to ring with cries for His blood, with mockery too, yet weeping over the beloved city, no resentment, no bitterness against those who thus were bringing their own destruction upon themselves, only sorrow for the shame of Israel—we see the perfection of divine compassion and pity. And, too, as our thoughts go forward to the last great day, when He shall sit upon the Great White Throne, and heaven and earth shall flee from His presence, we may be sure that He who pronounces the awful doom upon those who have refused His salvation, mocked at His entreaties and persistently identified themselves with all that was wicked, will have no feeling of triumph, but one of infinite, divine sorrow.

We dare not intrude beyond what God has revealed, but we know Him whose judgment is His "strange work," and who would fain warn men from that judgment. Over the abode of the lost, there will rest, we may be sure, in the heart of Him who was once the "Man of sorrows," even in all His glory, no thought but that which is consistent with those tears which He shed over Jerusalem. How hopeless, then, must be that state which can call forth only divine sorrow!

Little remains to be said of David's elegy in detail. "The beauty of Israel is slain upon thy high places: how are the mighty fallen." The flower of Israel was its king, one who had stood out in personal beauty above all his fellows. The heights of Israel should have been strongholds which no power of the enemy could assail; but how have the mighty fallen! All the power, and the beauty, and the greatness of men was here laid in the dust. As he thinks of this overthrow, David would fain draw the curtain over the scene, and hide from the gloating eyes of their enemies this scene of desolation: "Tell it not in Gath; publish it not in the streets of Ashkelon, lest the daughters of the Philistines rejoice, lest the daughters of the uncircumcised triumph."

Faith would ever remember that even judgment on Saul will bring no victory to other evil doers. The enemies of God shall gain no real triumph from the overthrow of human righteousness or excellence.

The mountains of Gilboa, where Saul and Jonathan fell, are to be cut off from all future blessing; neither dew nor rain are to fall upon them, nor are there to be fields which are to yield their flocks as offerings. It was the scene of death and judgment, an Aceldama, we may say, the place for the burial of strangers. For was it not here that the shield of the mighty was cast away—a shield without the oil of the Spirit's power.

There is remembrance of Saul's prowess in battle. He had indeed slain his thousands, and his sword had not returned empty from his conflict, as over Ammon, for instance. There is thus the recognition of what he had done, coupled with the bow of Jonathan. Then a sweet word follows; all, alas, that could be said that was common in the lives of Jonathan and Saul. They were lovely and pleasant in their lives, the link between father and son was not broken. Filial affection remained, even when Jonathan was compelled to refuse the conduct of his father, and in their death they were not divided. Losing sight for the time, of Jonathan's sharing in the defeat which we may be justified in connecting with what some have called a course of neutrality, David singles out this one point that he and his father fell together. He has only words of praise for their swiftness and courage in fight.

Then the sweet singer turns to the daughters of Israel who have suffered in the loss of their king. They must not forget that it was he who protected them and made possible their festive garments and other delights, their gold and apparel. There is just a glimpse at all this, and then again the dirge falls back to its theme: "How are the mighty fallen in the midst of the battle!"

But now, the eye of love turns to his own dear friend, the one whom he loved as his own soul. Jonathan had been slain in his high places. The one who had so valiantly climbed up into the high places, single-handed, to meet the whole proud host of the Philistines, is here a victim. As he thinks of him, David's heart gushes out with fresh sorrow. What exquisite beauty in these words: "I am distressed for thee, my brother Jonathan: very pleasant hast thou been unto me; thy love to me was wonderful."

Thank God, love remains, and this love of David to Jonathan has not upon it the cloud of hopeless sorrow which rests over his father. It is that which has lived throughout the ages, which has furnished a model of human friendship stronger than that of Damon and Pythias, a love tenderer than that of lovers, sweeter than that of women, the love of two strong, manly hearts, sanctified by a divine love; and to think that all true Christian friendship, even though for the time it be called to weep, has in it a perpetuity which can never be lost; and above all, how good it is that He of whom David was type is not ashamed to own His beloved people as friends; how surpassing, how wonderful, how tender is His love! Thank God, we shall never be called to mourn over the cessation of that!

Thus concludes your book.

Be sure to visit us online for more of the best Christian books ever written.

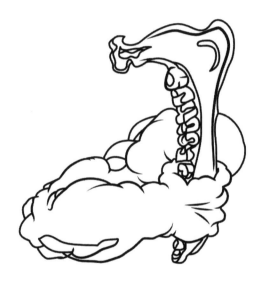

http://JawboneDigital.com

35902990R00130

Printed in Poland
by Amazon Fulfillment
Poland Sp. z o.o., Wrocław